CHARIF EL HAMRAOUI

Does ISIS contribute to preserving US supremacy ?

Let's see beyond the head lines

Does ISIS contribute to preserving US supremacy ?

" Power is the ability to influence the behaviour of others to get the outcomes one wants "
Joseph Nye,
Soft power : the means to success in World Politics

Does ISIS contribute to preserving US supremacy ?

Contents

5. US: the best safeguard of freedom of expression

    a. Ban of terrorism speech is unconstitutional and contrary to American history

    b. In front of the world, US preserve its ethic and spread its sights.

    c. A smart use of censorship

6. Well instrumented, ISIS fight is a differentiation element

    a. A game of cat and mouse; the white house and Congress

    b. Orlando shooting raises a critical juncture of the second amendment

    c. Pentagon, white house: a sneaky cooperation

    d. GOP presidential primaries have shown that two schools of thought emerge and will likely dispute.

7. ISIS: A crisis which will last.

    a. An enemy much tougher than thought

    b. Eagerness to kill VS willingness to die.

Bibliography

ISIS from an outcome to an asset

Does ISIS contribute to preserving US supremacy ?

At a time when we are witnessing a confrontation between those accusing the US and its agencies of creating ISIS and those treating the latter of silly conspiracy adepts, the truth may lie in a reality far more complex.

Tired of the long war, the US made its exit strategy.

Baghdad, 2006: America is facing the highest losses since it invades Iraq. The US's Military officers realize that the war would be a "long war" and therefore urge the pentagon to identify in which ways it might unfold and mostly how to get out of it.

From that point on, a prospective mission is entrusted to the Rand corporation, a non-profit research organization specialized in providing objective analysis and effective solutions. Its aim, to help the military to better assess the range of force sizes and the structures that it may need to develop to fight the war, the Rand Corp defined the unfolding of the long war.

The organization identified a number of trends and uncertainties associated with the future combat environment. This analysis, combined with its understanding of the components of the long war, provided the basis for a set of seven strategy options for the United States throughout this war.

Among these, there was the likes of divide and Rule, Shrink the Swamp, Inside Out or even Contain and React, These were, at that time, presented as pure options; probably part of hybrid approach.

Although not clear, the one that has been mostly advised was the " Divide and rule" option.

An option that has been found as the most suitable way to first narrow the threat on US interests and second, create a sustained

Sunni-Shia Conflict that which constitute an inexpensive way of buying time for the united states.

Indeed , It was thought that next hazard would come from elsewhere and could need probably time to dealt with. America understood well that while she would continue to act as the sole superpower, new major powers might emerge and increase in importance. Powers like China and India, which may pose a challenge on an economic basis and spark an arms race in the near future.

Narrowing the threat on US interest.

Identified as a trend, the advice to get it taken was for US to focus on exploiting fault lines between the various Salafi-jihadist groups to turn them against each other and dissipate their energy in internal conflicts.

And what a better way to do this than to confront the nationalist jihadists against the transnational ones.

Actually, this has been inspired from an already existing conflict in Iraq between al-Qaeda and the major tribal groupings.

Indeed there were clear ideological splits that could emerge. Increasingly public and vociferous; they could be found in a number of key issues, including the treatment of Shiites, the legitimacy of targeting civilians, a legitimacy of suicide operations, the utility of targeting oilfields in the Muslim world, or even on the way to win the hearts and minds of the Muslim population at large.

Mainly helped by the Middle Eastern political instability, and the capabilities of non-state actors, first illustration of US attempts appeared from the beginning of 2007 when many Iraqi Sunnis, approached by US agencies, started criticizing Al Qaida affiliate in Iraq for the foreign presence in its leadership and fighting forces as well as its attempts to impose its own radical brand of Islam on Iraqis through the use of extreme violence.

To get out of it, Masri, top commander, tried to brand the group as more Iraqi declaring the establishment of the Islamic State of Iraq. However, even if the name and leadership were be changed to seem as more Iraqi ("Baghdadi" means "from Baghdad"), several dissidents questioned whether Baghdadi truly ran the organization, or was just a figurehead.

It was not until 2011, when Abu Bakr al-Baghdadi (not to be confused with the deceased, Abu Umar al-Baghdadi) assumed control of an ISI severely weakened by local backlash, that US got real outcomes : Sunni attacks against Shiite targets increased in Iraq and elsewhere Osama bin Laden viewed global jihad as more of a long game, ISI focused on creating an Islamic state with established frontier and abiding sharia law.

Actually, The Islamic State, never expected to follow Al Qaeda's "far enemy" strategy, preferring instead the "near enemy" strategy, based on a regional level. As such, the primary target of the Islamic State has not been the United States, but rather apostate regimes in the Arab world—namely, Shia community in Iraq, Syria and Iran.

There resulted, in-line with US expectations, a war between two of the largest terrorist organizations in Iraq. As matter of fact, very recently, an Al-Qaeda linked group launched a surprise assault on the Islamic State.

Sustained Sunni-Shia Conflict: a slight helping hand was sufficient.

It must be said that there was a breeding ground for that.

Poor governance have always been exacerbating by the ideological tension resulting of the many conservative Sunni regimes in the Muslim world whom have discriminated systematically against Shiites for years.

In Saddam's Iraq, for example, all of the top positions in the Ba'ath Party, the military, and the intelligence services were reserved for

Sunnis even though Shiites are more than 50 percent of the total Iraqi population. Sunni areas of Iraq received more modern hospitals, schools, and roads than did Shia districts, where the infrastructure was usually allowed to decay.

In Saudi Arabia, Shiites had long faced restrictions on their celebration of religious festivals and have often been forbidden to construct new mosques. Schools in Shiite areas are now run by Sunni administrators which teach students that Shiism is illegitimate.

However and despite all these signals, Rand corp advised to not leave destiny in the long war uncontrolled. It suggested to America to walk a diplomatic tightrope on which it would have to maintain a strong strategic relationship with the Iraqi Shiite government while at the same time buttressing the conservative Sunni regimes in the Middle East that view the Iraqi regime as a challenge to the established order.

An advise that has not been taking lightly: while a simple boost was expected, America ignited a fire, giving all liberty in Iraq to Al Maliki, a Shiite representative and ensuring the start of a de-baathification process.

Indeed If it became evident that the Sunnis in Iraq could be permanently consigned to a second-tier political status, there would be considerable anxiety among many Sunni populations and clerics in the Arab world, who in turn feared spreading Shiite influence in their own countries.

An anxiety that would lead for sure to a proxy war financed by both parties : Saudi Arabia in one side, Iran in the other.

Also according to rand corp, "One of the oddities of this long war trajectory is that it may actually reduce the al-Qaeda threat to U.S. interests in the short term. The upsurge in Shia identity and confidence seen here would certainly cause serious concern in the Salafi-jihadist community in the Muslim world, including the senior leadership of al-Qaeda. As a result, it is very likely that al-Qaeda might focus its efforts on targeting Iranian interests throughout the Middle East and Persian Gulf while simultaneously cutting back on anti-American and anti-Western operations"

Such tendency if revealed, would allow a sub-sentential decrease of the US army footprint, the army would in turn be able to reduce its presence. A role which could be limited to some foreign internal defence missions to train host nation's security forces with possible insertion of advisers, but this might be in turn handled by other agencies. At the latter level, the U.S. Army would call upon rapid precision strike systems and would have to balance aggressive operations with an information campaign.

More stunning even, more America would appear to be politically weak, more likely the Middle East would move toward the Shia-Sunni conflict trajectory. Indeed, this would allow the USA some space to regain its regional reputation if America is able to regain its regional reputation, U.S. diplomatic pressure would by ethics, force local regimes to use the necessary mixes of carrots and sticks to stop sectarian conflict.

No way to deny, America knew about ISIS.

With the benefit of hindsight, ISIS appears to be one of the outcomes of such strategy. an outcome which turns out to be a perfect asset to the conduct and combat which had been advised.

After all, ISIS is not more than a national terror group that fights the Transnational Al Qaida and sustains the seemingly unavoidable Sunni Shia conflict.

But it's one thing to speculate; it's something entirely different to have hard proof. But this may all have changed now:

America's Allies are funding ISIS.

First Critics of the US-led regional strategy began raising questions about the intentional role of coalition allies in providing extensive support to Islamist terrorist groups driven to destabilize the Assad regime in Syria.

The conventional wisdom is that the US government did not retain sufficient oversight on the funding to anti-Assad rebel groups, which was supposed to be monitored and vetted to ensure that only 'moderate' groups were supported.

Indeed a key component of ISIS's support came from wealthy individuals in the Arab Gulf States of Kuwait, Qatar and Saudi Arabia for whom ISIS was a part of the Sunni forces locked in sectarian struggle with Shia forces. They considered themselves to be in an existential battle with both the Iranian backed Maliki government and the Assad regime

According to the December 2013 report by The Brookings Institution, a Washington think tank that receives some funding from the Qatari government, donors had taken advantage of Kuwait's weak financial rules and poor money laundering protections to channel hundreds of millions of dollars to a host of Syrian rebel brigades.

"Over the last two and a half years, Kuwait has emerged as a financing and organizational hub for charities and individuals supporting Syria's myriad rebel groups," the report said. "Today, there is evidence that Kuwaiti donors have backed rebels who have committed atrocities and who are either directly linked to al-Qaida or cooperate with its affiliated brigades on the ground."

The U.S. Treasury was also aware of this activity and has expressed concern about this flow of private financing. But Western diplomats' and officials' general response has been a collective shrug.

It was not until 2014 that Several US government officials have conceded that their closest allies in the anti-ISIS coalition were funding violent extremist Islamist groups that became integral to ISIS.

US Vice President Joe Biden, in person, admitted last year that Saudi Arabia, the UAE, Qatar and Turkey had funneled hundreds of millions of dollars to Islamist rebels in Syria that metamorphosed into ISIS.

However, all this does not provide evidence to determine if the US predetermined the current course of events in the middle east.

Now, thanks to a declassified report, the world has a far better understanding of not only how current events in the middle east came to be, but what America's puppet master role was, leading up to it all.

DIA declassified report : US "created" ISIS and envisions it as a strategic asset.

Indeed, a recent declassified secret US government document obtained by the public interest law firm, Judicial Watch, shows that Western governments deliberately allied with al-Qaeda and other Islamist extremist groups to topple Syrian dictator Bashar al-Assad. the newly declassified Pentagon report proves unambiguously that years before ISIS launched its concerted offensive against Iraq, the US intelligence community was fully aware that Islamist militants constituted the core of Syria's sectarian insurgency.

Despite that, the Pentagon continued to support the Islamist insurgency, even while anticipating the probability that doing so would lead to establishing an extremist Salafi stronghold in Syria and Iraq

Given the political leanings of the organization (judicial watch) that obtained the documents, it's unsurprising that the main emphasis given to files thus far has been an attempt to embarrass Hilary Clinton in the light the attack on the US consulate in Benghazi in 2012. However, the documents also contain far less publicized revelations that raise vitally important questions of the US strategy.

The newly declassified DIA document from 2012 confirms that the main component of the anti-Assad rebel forces by that time comprised Islamist insurgents affiliated to groups that would in turn lead to the emergence of ISIS. Despite this, these groups were to continue receiving support from Western militaries and their regional allies.

Noting that "the Salafist [sic], the Muslim Brotherhood, and AQI [al-Qaeda in Iraq] are the major forces driving the insurgency in Syria," the document states that "the West, Gulf countries, and Turkey support the opposition," while Russia, China and Iran "support the [Assad] regime."

The 7-page DIA document report notes that the "rise of the insurgency in Syria" has increasingly taken a "sectarian direction," attracting diverse support from Sunni "religious and tribal powers" across the region.

In a section titled 'The Future Assumptions of the Crisis,' the DIA report predicts that while Assad's regime will survive, retaining control over Syrian territory, the crisis will continue to escalate "into proxy war."

In a strikingly prescient prediction, the Pentagon's document explicitly forecasts the probable declaration of "an Islamic State through its union with other terrorist organizations in Iraq and Syria."

The secret Pentagon document thus provides extraordinary confirmation that the US-led coalition currently fighting ISIS, had three years ago welcomed the emergence of an extremist "Salafist Principality" in the region as a way to undermine Assad, and block off the strategic expansion of Iran. Crucially, Iraq is explicitly labelled as an integral part of this "Shia expansion."

Further on, the document reveals that Pentagon analysts were acutely aware of the dire risks of this strategy, yet regardlessly ploughed ahead.

The 2012 DIA document is an Intelligence Information Report (IIR), not a "finally evaluated intelligence" assessment, but its contents are vetted before distribution. The report was circulated throughout the US intelligence community, including to the State Department, Central Command, the Department of Homeland Security, the CIA, FBI, among other agencies.

This also suggests a decision to spend years deliberately mislead the West's public, via a compliant media, into believing that Syria's rebellion was overwhelmingly 'moderate.'

Throughout the early years of the Syrian crisis, the US and UK governments, and almost universal West's mainstream media, promoted Syria's rebels as moderate, liberal, secular, democratic, and therefore deserving of the West's support. Given that these documents wholly   undermine this assessment, it must be understood as significant that western media has now, despite their immense significance, almost entirely ignored them.

In conclusion, the revelations contradict the official line of Western government on their policies in Syria, and raise disturbing questions about secret Western support for violent extremists abroad, while using the burgeoning threat of terror to justify excessive mass surveillance and crackdowns on civil liberties at home.

Within NATO, a wolf in sheep's clothing: Turkey a state sponsor of ISIS.

New evidence has emerged that the Turkish government under Erdogan's Presidency is covertly providing direct military, financial and logistical support to ISIS, while claiming to be fighting the terror network.

The evidence comes in the form of a testimony from an ISIS fighter captured by Kurdish fighters who in an interview with ANHA (Kurdish press Agency), confessed that leading Turkish ISIS members move freely between Turkey and Syria because some of them are working for Turkish intelligence.

Border outposts would be routinely disbanded of Turkish security forces between particular arranged hours to allow groups of 20–30 ISIS fighters to pas unhindered and undetected.

Several other ISIS defectors have confirmed that ISIS field captains and commanders in Syria were in direct contact with "Turkish officials", as there was "full cooperation with the Turks.

According to Pentagon counter-terrorism consultant, Professor Anne Speckhard of Georgetown University, "Despite Erdogan's claims that he is fighting ISIS, evidence indicates that he has been, and continues to be, deeply complicit in allowing ISIS to transport, not just recruits via Turkey, but also weapons and supplies. These chilling facts have been confirmed over and again during our ISIS defector interviews. A former emir told us that ISIS had been able to construct thousands of propane tank bombs from supplies they brought in through Turkey."

But perhaps the most damning assessment was made by one of Erdogan's own allies, King Abdullah of Jordan, who told a meeting of senior Congressional representatives in Washington DC in January that Turkey was deliberately encouraging ISIS to dispatch terrorists across the border into Europe, to carry out terrorist attacks.

Abdullah also confirmed that the Turkish state was complicit in ISIS oil sales. President Erdogan, he said, was committed to a "radical Islamic solution to the region" and to the conflict in Syria.

Do US really want ISIS to be defeated?

Does ISIS contribute to preserving US supremacy ?

Nothing but reprisals and spin, US refuse to bear the burden.

Looking to any western media, No one can deny that united states is fighting ISIS, but it's one thing to fight a terror group, it is something else to take the means to defeat it.

Even if US had have been blamed in the past and in purpose for being "effectively blind", Obama, since beginning of that year decided to contend ISIS and that started by airstrikes on oil sites and on cash depots in ISIS-land resulting on the incineration of more than half-a-billion dollars.

This aggressiveness was partly in response to the ISIS-directed and inspired attacks in Paris and San Bernardino, which showed ISIS's violent influence was metastasizing faster than the administration expected.

After more than a year of reluctance to target the terrorist's core infrastructure for fear of hitting civilians or risking the lives of American troops, the entire dynamic has changed: the resilience to risk civilian casualties has been growing and military commanders have been asked to not hold back anymore and show their ideas.

Indeed, White House started encouraging military planners to widen the strike zone whom previously had been targeting within Iraq and Syria had been limited mostly to identifiable ISIS checkpoints and safe houses in remote areas. In other words, we now tolerate collateral damages in the interest of making progress.

First illustration of that shift: the signing by the secretary of state, Ashton carter in January, of two cash depot targets ordered by Central Command.

the bank strikes combined with targeting the oil infrastructure had produced a serious cash crunch. ISIS fighter morale has plummeted and foreign fighters started deserting because salaries have been halved, according to some U.S. officials. ISIS has since moved much of the remaining cash to a hospital in Mosul, the officials said.

Unfortunately, all that was just mater of reprisals. Faced with the practical impossibility to dispatch more elite forces until proves were given of the worth of the ones already sent, Secretary of state once again reiterated appeals to coalition partners asking them to step up their contributions to core resources.

An appeal that remains by the way an ongoing point of contention: for many military commanders, capping the U.S. troops to less than 4,000 in Iraq, and relying on other coalition partners for other tasks to keep U.S. numbers down, creates an unwieldy patchwork of training and logistics.

All the more so as Saudi Arabia and the United Arab Emirates do not have the capabilities to contribute significantly to the fight against the Islamic State in Iraq and Syria.

Even if both the UAE and Saudi Arabia express their willing to engage on the ground upon U.S. leadership, questions linger over whether either country's troops would be effective.

"Whether they have the capacity to do both Yemen and something in Iraq-Syria is questionable for me," said Vincent Stewart, director of the Defence Intelligence Agency . "I think they're doing extremely well in Yemen, but their capacity to do more is pretty limited."

Actually, such outcome of the DIA, the agency best able to provide field reports, have been seen as a request for more U.S. ground troops.

A reconsideration that has led the white house to unleash America's elite hunter-killer forces against ISIS.

Military commanders started then drafting plans for U.S. troops to accompany Iraqi brigades as they move to retake Mosul, plans where more soldiers would have to be much closer to the front lines of what was expected to be a fierce battle for Iraq's second largest city.

But meanwhile Iraqi commanders estimate the Mosul offensive will take between eight to twelve brigades — which would mean the engagement of approximately 180 U.S. troops, the new plan would see small US. teams of about 15 troops which would work on ordering airstrikes, and providing intelligence, logistics, tactics, and fire support.

This restraint is due to the fact that moving closer to the front would certainly expose US troops to more risk.

"The risk is you move off these protected forward operating bases and these troops could be, not just killed, but kidnapped," said Peter Mansoor, retired Army colonel, adding "There are plenty of Shiite militias that would be happy to take American service members captive."

Moreover, this would be out of touch with the lesson learned from previous middle east conflicts. "The distinction we've laid out there from a policy standpoint is, we don't want the service members to be the number one man through the door," explained the newest U.S. special operations commander, using the example of Army Master Sgt. Joshua L. Wheeler, who was killed while helping Kurdish forces liberate an ISIS prison in Northern Iraq.

America soldiers are trying desperately to work through other people, have them do their own security as much as they can, so as to shield their nation from bearing the burden.

Meanwhile in Syria, the situation is much more complicated, there is no army to train, no military staff to collaborate with as the departure of Assad and its army is an essential prerequisite of each cooperation.

There are just rebels groups and Kurdish militia to work with. These insurgents have been at the beginning of the civil war the subjects of a Syrian rebel programs initiated by the CIA. However, most of them joined the different terror group considered more effective.

Now lawmakers are skeptical of restarting rebel program: according to the hill, the newspapers in charge of covering the congress, the push to restart the Pentagon's program to train Syrian rebels to fight the Islamic State in Iraq and Syria (ISIS) is facing early opposition from senators.

Congressmen are voicing deep concern that a second attempt by the Pentagon would amount to little more than misspent tax dollars or, at worst, would bolster ISIS by giving them easy access to U.S. equipment.

Even if pentagon officials ensured that any reboot of the program would include changes aimed at avoiding the missteps that led to the program being shut down last year, even if it has been told to senators that the new program would include shorter training and "focus on smaller numbers of people that we can train on specific skills", the train-and-assist thing was not the right way to go in the minds of the foreign relation committee.

It must be said that it was a difficult pill to swallow. As early as 2014, Congress approved $500 million for the Syrian train-and-equip program 2014 despite same deep concerns in both chambers about the strategy and the resolve of Syrian moderate rebel fighters.

Even though, political pragmatism prevailed. Indeed faced with democrats that support their president and republicans that must show their bellicosity, no one would have resisted the Pentagon especially that the institution was happy to report that the results were to be see.

Secretary of Defence tells anyone who could stand to hear it again that the US strategy are delivering the intended results. The endless airstrikes combined with the local troops urged ISIS to lose 45 percent of the territory it once held in Iraq and 20 percent of areas it controlled in Syria, according to U.S.-led coalition current estimates.

These gains coincide with a string of terror bombings in and around Baghdad this year. In just the past week, 200 people were killed. Targeting Shiite neighborhoods in order to trigger a larger conflict between the two Muslim factions, ISIS seems to return to its roots.

The so called, Islamic state, does not resemble anymore to the conventional military forces know earlier, the one that operated in large formations and employed heavy weapons. The militants now move in smaller groups and retreat from some of the territory they controlled. "Their ability to conduct large-scale offensive operations has primarily stopped," said Army Maj. Gen. Gary Volesky, a top commander in Iraq.

Affirmation that should be taken with a grain of salt, in view of the recent revelations by central command analysts which claimed that intelligence reports were manipulated to make it appear that the U.S. war is going better than some analysts think it is

Actually, US CentCom, theater-level Unified Combatant Command in charge of the middle east, is embroiled in climate of fear. Analysts are suspicious of their bosses, and bosses are suspicious of the analysts

In interviews, half a dozen current and former officials have described the environment at CENTCOM headquarters as "toxic" and "hostile" owing to a long-simmering dispute over whether political influence was brought to bear on intelligence analysts whose job is to objectively assess the strength of ISIS and the effects of the U.S.-led efforts to destroy the group.

They say the written and verbal pressure created a climate at CENTCOM in which analysts felt they had to self-censor some of their reports reaching conclusions favored by their bosses but not supported by facts.

Analysts allegations concern also senior officials accuse to delete emails and files that would show they more heavily edited reports that took a dimmer view of U.S. efforts to combat ISIS.

Weak and disabled, Pentagon strategy relies on untrusted partners.

Widely criticized as ineffective, especially after ISIS fighters seized the city of Ramadi in May 2015, a new approach has been drafted beginning of this year.

The new plan calls for fighting the terror group like a conventional enemy, relying on traditional military tactics such as maneuver-style warfare and attrition, a move clearly depicted through the new appointment of an army stalwart as the first flag officer to oversee all anti-ISIS operations.

Having a more conventional background than its predecessor, his plans would have require more Americans on the ground but again political considerations come into play and plead for the use of a dizzying patchwork of local untrusted partners.

So far, the plan consists on making the local ground troops, mainly Kurdish and Iraqi, moving in large formations to isolate and ultimately invade the two major ISIS strongholds: Mosul in Iraq and Raqqa in Syria.

Indeed by severing the ISIS supply line between the two hottest cities, pentagon strategists hope to carve up the group's territory into smaller pockets that can be defeated through isolation and direct assault.

According to army Brig. Gen. Mark Odom, the top U.S. commander in Iraq's Kurdish region, this strategy is affordable as this began already with the November attack on Sinjar in Iraq's northwest. Though ISIS continues to move some supplies between the two cities using secondary roads, these are really in very poor condition cutting their previous ability to resupply.

Second mainstay is the cut-off of the Islamic State's primary feeder lines to the outside world by pressuring the border states and mainly Turkey to seal its border as it is through Turkey's southern border that Islamic State replenishes itself in terms of money, weapons and people.

However even if approved and probably winning, the main worry of this plan lies mostly in the fact that it involves many partners often with competing agendas.

First example of this objection: The Iraqi refusal of US support for the recent fight in Ramadi, a clear sign that anti-American politics in Baghdad may limit the U.S. military's ability to operate inside Iraq.

As matter of fact, whereas US were offering to magnify the effectiveness of their airstrikes and real-time intelligence capabilities, Iraqi leaders began imposing restrictions on the size and scope of the U.S. military force in their country. Factions within Baghdad's Shiite-led government are currently influenced by neighboring Iran and thus oppose expanding the American military mission there.

"Iraq is proving to be a lot trickier than we thought," said Michael Knights, a military expert within the Washington Institute for Near East Policy. "You've always got the risk that you can unbalance the government if you do too much. ... We've learned that it can be a lot simpler operating in an environment where you have no sovereign government [like Syria] than to operate in a place where you've got one, like in Iraq."

The second objection came that time from the Syrian Kurdish militia, who, gathered in political organization, have announced the constitution of an autonomous federation in the northern part of Syria.

According to Taj Kordsh, a spokesman for the Syrian Democratic Forces," Kurdish feel that the world powers are using them as a tool to push forward their agendas. It is now their right to protect themselves. Kurdish do not support dividing Syria, but expect an equal and fair outcome from the peace talks, and they have not seen any."

This move has been done in party to anger neighboring Turkey, an another American asset in that war.

Indeed, Turkish leaders have been engaged for many decades in a conflict with its own Kurdish minority. They fear that growing Kurdish power in Syria would encourage separatism ambitions amongst its own minority, a fear that may push Turkey to change its priorities and deliberately fail to seal its border.

In other words and to make it short, America relies in its fight on two competing actors, who see on ISIS as the most suitable asset to defend its own interests.

Aside the competing agendas, pentagon strategy is furthermore at odds with its passed experience, military officials seem to not draw the lessons from the passed Middle east conflict.

While several analysts have repeatedly advised to consider ethnic identities in the battle plan for Syria, secretary of defense wait considerable time thinking that Syrian Kurds were ideal invasion forces for Raqqa, a Sunni Arab city.

It is only recently that US has figured out that it wants Arabs to do the job. According to Aron Lund, a Syria military expert, "US realize they need that. If they sent in this ultra-secular Kurdish group into a city of rather conservative Arab tribal groups, that would not work out very well." " The U.S. has tried to "play down" the SDF's Kurdish element and "make it into a multiethnic, multi-sectarian thing," Lund added. "They see that as being the only way to take Raqqa. But in reality, it's very clear that for the command and control for all of the offenses, the Kurds are doing this. It's the same Kurdish force doing the heavy lifting."

Constant change of allies delays the conflict's end.

Facing huge difficulties to find local forces on the ground of Syria, Pentagon is opening a batch of criticism at each change of allies, indeed at every change it delays the end of the conflict.

It was the hill that raised awareness among officials by publishing "US seems to standing by whiles its allies are killed"

Actually, since February 2016, the Obama administration is allowing moderate Syrians rebels, which the US spent hundreds of millions training and equipping, to be slowly destroyed: the groups are both targeted by Russians air strikes and new attacks for the Kurdish groups.

As matter of fact, Pentagon began a 500 million effort in 2014 to train moderate opposition rebels but the program struggled to find recruits who would only target ISIS and not the Syrian regime and was effectively ended after the US spent 384 million to field 145 fighters.

However aside this wasted money and the criticism that Obama faced because of its non-coherence, choosing YPG militia over "moderate rebels" raises many challenges for the end of the conflict.

Firstly, the Kurdish militia aspiration : for sure, they are by and large the only people who have been willing to fight ISIS in the ground of eastern Syria, however they have their own agenda, objective: they want to establish a Kurdish autonomous zone which is running relations with NATO ally Turkey since the YPG is closely linked to PKK, a group blamed by turkey for several bombing lately. the last statement to come from John Kerry who highlights that "supporting the Kurdish militia doesn't extend to its political goals, as US do no support some sort of semi-autonomous zone for Kurds" has failed to ease the developing tensions with Turkey.

Secondly, YPG are supporting Russia and Assad regime, against the rebels by providing the coordinates of the rebels headquarters in northern Syria.

In other words, U.S. Central Command's principal ground force against ISIS in northern Syria, the Kurdish People's Protection Units, have taken to attacking CIA-backed Sunni Arab rebels as the latter were pounded by Russia bombs.

There has been, by the way, a symbolic benefit for the Russian General Staff of watching as the U.S. waged a proxy war against itself.

Last but not least, the sense of betrayal felt by Mainstream Syrian rebels. Not standing for the Syrian rebels sends a message to other allies that the US cannot be trusted: and that's without even talking about how the Europeans are affected by this.

America is fully aware that the collaboration of Sunnis inside ISIS stronghold positions is essential to defeat the terror group, nevertheless, such move from their part would affect ,for sure, the predisposal of hostage population to collaborate.

ISIS fight: a fresh reboot to the US's economical Supremacy.

Does ISIS contribute to preserving US supremacy ?

Defence lobby and its conduct of psychological warfare to gain population support in the US.

As in all modern wars conducted under USA hegemony, the psychologic aspect takes a considerable place. In order to gain the population support, defence lobbies through military officials and political figures intensify what can be assimilated to propaganda.

Indeed, aiming to build-up a national concern, what better way to do it than referring to the whiff of the Vietnam war. And again what better way to do this than making appeal to the most popular vet : John Mc Cain.

Intended to Defense Secretary Ashton Carter, the Senate Armed Services Committee Chairman compared in a letter the White House's current strategy in the Middle East to the "failed policy of gradual escalation" reached in the Vietnam War. "the US fight is starting to become an "another slow and grinding failure".

In a tentative to put pressure on the white house, he added that its conversations with military commanders both on the ground and in the Pentagon have led him to the disturbing, yet unavoidable conclusion, that they have been reduced from considering what it will take to win to what they will be allowed to do by this administration."

He maintained that a more accurate accounting of the military's footprint there is needed to "provide the necessary resources and support America war fighters need to achieve their missions and return home safely."

This attack is baffling at the very least, because the very same one has been used by democrats at capitol hill for exactly the opposite 8 years ago. Indeed during the last war in Iraq, Democrats on Capitol Hill invoked as well the Vietnam War comparison when pressing then-President George W. Bush for an exit strategy from the region.

Afraid to be outdone, the chairman of the House Armed Services Committee, Mac Thornberry, also criticized the US strategy, a strategy that does not look for victory but for avoiding disaster.

"I think what you've seen is the president just slowly dialling up the pressure: A few hundred more people; a slight relaxation of the rules on when they can drop bombs," said Rep. Mac Thornberry. "It's not really to win."

Actually, Largely funded by Northrop Grumman, an American global aerospace and defence technology company, the Texas senator does not understand the large cuts in the defense spending. For him, the pentagon's budget became a politic football between republicans that don't want to increase spending at all for anything and democrats who look for increase only on the domestic side and who's caught in the middle? It's the men and women who serve.

With the aim of getting closer to the ordinary citizen, Thornberry does not hesitate to use storytelling. Indeed, the lawmaker insisted on how budget cuts have affected service members lives.

"I've talked to a top pilot for one of the services who's leaving the service — loves what he does — but he doesn't think the aircraft he flies are safe anymore and he's got two young kids at home."

The houses have also done its part of the job, passing a legislation to formally classify violence committed by Islamic State militants against religious and ethnic minorities as genocide.

The resolution, passed easily on a vote of 393-0, had as a purpose to raise the international consciousness and compel the responsibility communities of the world to act.

The words as slavery, beheadings, human trafficking and torture, among other atrocities were often relayed by the press and featured on the Internet.

Even though such designation would have significant consequences as the establishment of a Syrian war crimes tribunal, the congress persisted treating the ISIS persecution toward Christians, Yazidis and other religious and ethnic minorities as crimes against humanity.

Military Industry : a reboot of non US sales.

Relying on the international coalition to arm local groups as well as on ISIS to sustain an endless Sunni-Shia conflict, Obama's government ensure a bright future for defence companies.

Today, most valuable defence lobby groups are CSP and APPS.

While CSP, Washington-based think tank has lost its credibility because of the nature of its donators (Lockheed Martin and Raytheon), American for Peace Prosperity and Security appears now as the new pressure group. Founded by former FBI agent Mike Rodgers, it was formed in the run-up to the presidential election of 2016 with the stated aim of helping to "elect a president who supports American engagement and a strong foreign policy.

The slogan for APPS is keeping "America safe" however, a quick look at its leadership board suggests that securing the business interest could also be a driving factor behind the group. Recent research shows that of seven (7) members of APPS's national advisory board, three (3) have strong business links with defence companies (BAE systems, Insight Technology ...), and stand to gain financially if the US pursues same foreign policy line post 2016.

Now that domestic defence spending knows radical cutbacks, defence firms are focusing on foreign customers, by far the most lucrative portion of the market and with tensions in the Middle East looking unlikely to subside any time soon, arms manufactures are among the primary beneficiaries of the incertitude.

Bloomberg news reported that non US Sales at the four leading US defence companies have climbed by 9 percent.

"The current conflict in Yemen and general tensions in the region will probably work to the benefit of arms companies," says Hartung, who heads CIP's Arms and Security Project. "The industry thrives on tensions."

Recently, a promotional video of the group describes the "treat matrix" facing the US and pledges to increase defence cooperation with allies in the middle east as an ultimate solution: an analysis that inevitably came to the President Obama who promised to fast-track arms transfers to Gulf cooperation countries states which are contributing to regional security.

With no further ado, Raytheon and Lockheed Martin, main US-based defence manufactures, announce a new arms export contract for the sales of missiles worth $ 1.75 bn to Saudi Arabia which is currently taking part in anti-coalition strikes in Syria alongside the US.

Saudi Arabia and the United Arab Emirates were among the world's five biggest arms importers in 2012-2013. In their 2013 annual report, BAE Systems noted that "in Saudi Arabia, regional tensions continue to dictate that defence remains a high priority." despite military spending cut-backs in Europe and North America, "spending in the Middle East...is expected to drive the military...market for the foreseeable future."

Indeed, there is no hope that tensions would be subsided. As the US began bombing IS sites in Syria on September 2015, concerns were raised that the campaign could ultimately aid the government of Syrian President Bashar al-Assad, which has been battling Saudi-funded rebels in the country since a 2011 uprising.

Indeed torn between its willing to defeat Shiites and preserve Sunni leadership, Saudi Arabia has long voiced fervent opposition to Assad's government, and has been involved in funding rebel groups throughout the drawn-out conflict.

Now that ISIS is developing quickly in their borders, Saudis decided to make shift in their regional strategy. It is a strategy that started in 2013 when the authorities began to adopt a hyper-active and highly risky policy of fighting Islamists in any way they can. It explains their support for the coup in Egypt in 2013, and it explains their support for the anti-IS coalition.

"They even deliberately confuse the Muslim Brotherhood and IS, portraying all Islamist groups as a major threat that has to be combatted. It is striking how we are now hearing exactly the same discourse in Riyadh and Cairo." Said Lacroix, assistant professor at Science Po in Paris

Though the anti-IS campaign will be a lengthy fight that could ultimately aid Saudi Arabia's arch rivals, like Iran and Syria's President Assad, Lacroix adds that Saudi's participation in the bombing is "a question of priorities in the end."

So combining Saudi Arabia all-out strategy to Obama willing to transfer US power to Asia, US defence firm's future shines bright.

Obama administration has approved more arms sales than any other US administration since world war II, sixty percent of these exports have gone to middle East and the Persian Gulf countries. Indeed, reforms to the export trade, which would see the responsibility for approving arms sales shifted from the state department to the commerce department, were pushed by the industry for decades.

Obama is definitely one of the greatest friends of the arms industry.

San Bernardino attack: US retake leadership over Tech moguls.

The San Bernardino terrorist attacks, gave the public at large a clearer idea of the encryption issue that face US intelligence agencies.

Indeed, behind the apparent fight between the FBI and Apple, what are really clashing, are the efforts made by the tech firms to protect their costumer's data and governments willing to spy terror group which clearly take advantages of these.

Let's remind the facts:

December 2, 2015, 14 people were killed and 22 were seriously injured in a terrorist attack at San Bernardino. Result of mass shooting and bomb attempt, investigation is entrusted to the FBI.

February 9, 2016, the FBI announced that it was unable to unlock one of the mobile phones he had recovered, an iPhone 5C owned by the shooter Farook. As a result, the FBI asked Apple who declined.

Criminals and terrorists, benefiting from the same protections as innocent consumers, they use these to shield their information and communications from law enforcement and intelligence agencies. This is part of the so called "going dark" problem.

Revealed as one of the major challenges for the future, End-to-end encryption made US Government torn between two approaches. Either, he takes the leadership and requests its access to these data or he collaborates with Californian tech moguls

As matter of fact, the end-to-end encryption issues have gone well beyond the framework of terrorism as the problem is also a drug trafficking, kidnaping and child pornography issue that impact every state of the union.

Let's have a look how US Government expects to deal with, probably by following its common way to proceed: First tackle, then temper and ultimately collaborate.

Venal and unethical, Apple is the company of choice for terrorists.

Right after the San Bernardino incident, The Californian firm started facing public attacks from republicans in congress who called on Apple to cooperate. According to them, it was unfortunate that a great company like Apple choose to protect a dead ISIS terrorist's privacy over the security of American people. Indeed according to the FBI, the phone could contain information valuable to its investigation.

Drawing the parallel with Paris terrorist attack, National Security Agency (NSA) Director Adm. Michael Rogers claimed that encryption had also helped the strikers hide from authorities before carrying out their deadly assault in November. "Some of their communications were encrypted," and as a result "we did not generate the insights ahead of time. Clearly, Paris would not had happened".

Actually, Paris is emblematic of a larger trend in which criminals and terrorists are using encryption to "go dark." Therefore, republican chieftains believe that companies should provide investigators with guaranteed access to secured data.

In the wake of these attacks, Apple is also blamed for regularly making concessions to the Chinese government while in parallel it refuses to help the FBI unlock the San Bernardino shooter's Iphone.

Actually for many experts, Apple has made without a doubt, slight concessions on some of its hard-line privacy positions in order to operate under china's strict internet regime. The tech firm had to move Chinese user data to Chinese government servers and install a different Wifi protocol. Made initially to comply with such tedious tech regulations, these deviations would make it easier for the authorities to hack into apple products. Indeed, it didn't took too long to see Beijing suspected of being behind malware used to spy Chinese iPhone users in 2014.

Outraged by such accusation and in effort to push back persecutors, the Californian brand argued that it had not weakened security in order to operate in China, but have done that just to improve the streaming quality of audio and video files, the key of local servers being kept in USA.

The tech firm claimed also that it complied rather with 81 % over of US government requests for data over 9000 devices which according to Tim Cook, its Chief executive officer (CEO), is a higher response rate on more than twice requests. It is just that the kind of information it has provided to Chinese authorities differs from what US federal agency is seeking to access on the terrorist phone. Beijing's request typically included information about account holder such as name and address not the user content like photos, emails or device back-ups. What a weak defence !

However, there is several reasons to be skeptical: indeed apple was only able to offer its flagship iPhone 6 in china after convincing Beijing that the smartphones met the country's strict Internet control standards as well as for its 4S version which has been modified for sale.

Moreover, the recent counter-terrorism Chinese laws demand that companies help authorities to decrypt data upon request and offer investigators assistance when necessary. While the law only applies on operator, and internet service providers, the vague wording could lay the groundwork to legally force apple to unlock I-phones in China.

Never mind, Let's temper the attacks in view of a probable partnership

The most stunning in this case is the first Apple's backing which came from United States Secretary of Defense Ashton Carter, himself, which made a noticeable effort to send a signal to techies.

For him, "US citizens need their data security and encryption to be as strong as possible. Future policy shouldn't be driven by any one particular case"

Even the national security agency (NSA) Director, Michael Rogers, also took it upon himself to explain that while encryption has hurt surveillance capabilities, this is one of the pillar of the modern society.

"Does encryption make it much more difficult for us to execute our mission. Yes. I acknowledge that encryption is foundational to the future", Rogers said

In short, Pentagon believes outlawing certain types of encryption, as some lawmakers have called for, is not the solution.

Californian tech firms undertook also a lobby action to stand behind Apple. They started acting through a former tech industry executive which is now at the congress, Suzan DelBene. Funded by Microsoft, she called the FBI moves as irresponsible solution to a complex problem. "It is not about a company and a single phone but we are asking to set a precedent that it says OK to force the companies to create new master keys to break into devices Americans rely on every day to handle sensitive information "

The tech users also claimed its position, insisting such access would introduce vulnerabilities into devices that could be exploited by hackers. As a result, basic digital privacy and common Internet activities such as online banking could be at risk, they say.

Indeed, while the government is insisting that requests is tailored to the single phone question, Apple and others have warned that complying would send a public signal to other countries including those with questionable human right records like china that such requests are fair game.

The company advanced that the standoff is expected to protracted legal battle that could determine the future of access encrypted services. by complying, technology companies would set a precedent that would endanger global encryption and online privacy.

Now on the verge of been defaced, Military should be careful with Silicon Valley recruitment.

The Apple-FBI standoff is coming at a bad time for the Pentagon. The Apple-FBI feud overshadowed two announcements out West, such as security experts gathered in San Francisco for RSA, the cybersecurity industry's largest annual conference.

Indeed, such controversy is threatening to undermine the Pentagon's attempt to recruit talent from Silicon Valley. It is obvious that if US implements a much harder line on encryption, the negotiation between Californian firms and US DOD will narrow.

Actually, we are assisting a broad push across the government to build ties to the centre of the tech industry. The Department of Homeland Security has opened accordingly a Silicon Valley office and President Obama held a daylong cybersecurity conference at Stanford University last year.

As matter of fact, the military is working on quickly ramping up a half-staffed U.S. Cyber Command, trying to fill more than 6,200 available positions.

In his wish to "rebuild bridges" which were badly damaged in 2013 after that the whistle-blower Edward Snowden exposed the extent of government spying. Carter became by the way, the first Defense chief to visit Silicon Valley in nearly two decades. He has since tallied three visits in 12 months and instigate the opening of the Pentagon's first ever offices in the Bay Area.

Pentagon unveiled two new programs that some security experts see as a major shift in how a secretary of defence approaches technology.

According to Kate Moussouris, a former hacker, it's the Pentagon "accepting the dark arts, accepting hackers' skills as something that is really important"

Of course surfing on such wave, Carter was not intending to stop here and conducted a second initiative: the creation of Pentagon advisory board headed by Eric Schmidt, the executive chairman of Google's parent company.

Carter "has a global perspective, he runs a global organization," McNerney, a former advisor of secretary of defense said. "He has to think about not just immediate tactical security issues, but also global transnational threats. failing to work together would risk letting others set the standard on their terms and according to their values.

Silicon Valley is receptive to the global perspective: It's even one of the main defences Apple, Google, Microsoft and others have used to justify their resistance to the FBI's call for help. They are afraid that no one will trust their products overseas and that nothing will stop any more other governments from asking for the same hacking assistance.

Indeed, there are unintended Consequence behind the End-to-End encryption, consequences that may affect US imperialism in cybersecurity

Actually, it is obvious that if the U.S. force Apple to do this, other countries, including less friendly countries, will start demanding that phone companies also provide them with a way around the encryption, and this workaround will not be used for good in some countries.

What happens if this new passcode-cracking software could be used to disable protections on many devices, Millions of devices go from being very secure to very vulnerable. Consumer cyber-security and privacy would take a huge blow, as would the reputation of American tech companies.

Even worse would be the encryption arms race generated by such precedent. If Apple creates this program for the FBI that breaks down passcode protections, nothing stops Apple from making those protections even harder or maybe even impossible to remove in their next update to their operating system or in the next iPhone. By the way, that is already the case on the newest apple products where passcode delay protection is seemingly impossible to remove.

pentagon is fully aware that being out of such race implies ill-considered risks. Working side by side with tech moguls and funding their research, are the only way to gain their cooperation on the one hand and ensure they remain the best.

Indeed there is a risk that America rivals would start using third-party apps like Telegram that encrypt communication. Mostly foreign, companies making these encryption programs are unlikely to help US intelligence agencies.

Now, only the future will tell us the outcome of Carter's moves, but for sure if the FBI is successful in its court battle against Apple, all bets are off.

ISIS presence: a 'tour de force' geo-economic

Does ISIS contribute to preserving US supremacy ?

Fear of internal terrorism and the defence of economic interests, lead china to its first foreign military involvement.

Kissinger once wrote once that Beijing follows the Chinese proverb that says "sitting atop of mountains to watch a fight between tigers". That's no longer the case anymore.

While much ink has been spilled by European analysts on Russia and Iran's support of Syria, several US reporters are speculating on China's motivations.

China has had strong trade relations with Syria in the past. Strong economic cooperation has been held with the Bashar al-Assad regime since 2001. After that both parties signed an agreement on economic and technical cooperation, China became Syria's third most important trading partner.

The same applies for military aspect: the People's republic worked hard to get as many weapons into Syria as Syria could afford, more or less ignoring U.S. protests. In April 2014 when Kafr Zita was hit with chlorine gas, evidence showed that the chlorine gas came from the state-owned company China North Industries (Norinco), the same company that denied any involvement in its gas selling to South Sudan, to a South Sudanese government well known for "razing entire villages, burning people alive, and raping children."

This ambiguous support, should the focus be made on china internal affairs and latest Xi Jinping visits, appears to be driven by various geopolitical and economic interests. To Imad Moustapha, Syria's ambassador to China, it boils down to three motivations: "international law and legitimacy; global strategic positioning; and the activities of jihadists Uighurs from Xinjiang province in China's far west"

Unlike the European union, China will not be confronted with an influx of refugees from the war-torn country. Nevertheless, Beijing has started to actively engage with both the Syrian government and opposition leaders in an apparent effort to mediate the conflict. The reasons for China's new approach are first the desire to be seen as an influential actor on the stage of global diplomacy.

China's unprecedented involvement in Syria is seen by President Xi jinxing as a diplomatic trial balloon. The Syrian peace process provides a unique opportunity for China's diplomats to broaden their experience with multilateral global crisis management and conflict mediation. "The ability to shape the resolution of international conflicts is central to Chinese president and party leader's vision of an assertive China taking on more international responsibilities, reflecting its status as a global power".

According to several geopolitical experts, one of the reason behind China using its veto, was to stand with Russia against what both consider to be the European and US autocracy deciding the fate of some regimes. People' republic is concerned about granting the west the green light to do whatever it likes with regards to toppling regimes and countries that may have an impact on Chinese interests.

Though china has less direct stake in Syria than Russia or US so far, the collapse of Syria will result in the west further controlling the Middle east, and Iran taking direct pressure from the West. Direct consequence: China would have to rely more on Russia for energy, bringing the uncertainty to the Sino-Russian strategic partnership.

Xi Jinping's state visits to Saudi-Arabia, Egypt, and Iran (January 19-23) — making the Middle East the last major world region for Xi to visit — also illustrated that China is willing to act as a diplomatic heavyweight in the Middle East and press the most urgent questions in the region. in Egypt, Xi openly addresses the Syrian issue and calls for a political solution of the conflict.

China's Foreign Minister Wang's announcement on December 18th, inviting representatives from both sides of the conflict to China, this did not came as a surprise. The time by when Beijing was expressing its reluctance to engage out of respect for Syria's sovereignty is over.

Further reason of this involvement: the lack of outlet faced by china. Marginalized by the past, years of economic success made the MENA region too important to ignore. Looking to maintain a manufacturing and construction-dominated economy, Middle eastern economies are some of the few remaining locales in which Chinese manufactured goods have not yet come to dominate the market.

During his visit, Xi put the most emphasis on promoting the China's first Arab Policy Paper. Coming as a check-book diplomat brokering deals, he focuses on increasing energy-cooperation and infrastructure investments as well as cooperation in the high-tech sector.

It must be said that MENA region is vital for China's global power aspirations. indeed, the latter has recently launched the One Belt, One road Initiative, a large web of infrastructure and trade connecting china to much of Asia, Africa and Europe through middle east.

However on-going fighting and terror attacks are putting this mega-project at risk, indeed Beijing's $900-billion Silk road initiative which aims to connect china through a wide ranging infrastructure network would have to cross all these countries. China is very apprehensive about the region's politics. Beijing observed the events of Arab spring with concern, particularly in how quickly regional stability eroded following revolutionary movements. China's leadership has no invest heavily in a state only to have that investment threatened by conflict. China needs the MENA region, but fears the direction the region may be turning.

Beyond the geopolitical or economic interests, there is also a key factor which western press largely omits: the linkage of Syria to stability in China's Muslim Xinjiang.

Since Damascus became a witch's brew of international jihadi fighters, China found itself facing a new threat: the internationalization of the Uyghurs' separatist cause forming in the crucible of the Syrian war. Chinese Uyghur separatists, a Turkic ethnic group living in Eastern china, practice Islam and have traditionally enjoyed support in Turkey. First signs of increasing linkage between localized separatist movements with global terrorist network appeared in 2011.

In the July 2011 Xinjiang bombings, for the first time Uyghur separatists planted a Salafist flag rather than their usual East

Turkestan flag. Uyghurs began proclaiming aspirations to join the Middle East jihadi movement, stoking China's fears that Uyghurs would garner global jihadist support from Al-Qaeda, and Al-Qaeda in the Islamic Maghreb, which attacked Chinese interests in Algeria in 2009, among others.

As Muslim brotherhood have seen the first Afghanistan guerrilla against soviets as a training field, Uyghurs are fighting in Syria alongside Al-Qaeda and other jihadists against the Assad regime, with the aim that the Xinjiang-Syrian jihadists would seriously undermine China's national security, as reported by Chinese press.

Beijing worries that if Assad falls and is replaced by an Islamist regime, extremism will quickly spread to the Muslim republics in Central Asia and destabilize China's backyard. Xinjiang already faced attacks by jihadists launched from Pakistan.

The territorial integrity of Muslim Xinjiang itself is a core interest for Beijing. It is one-sixth the size of China's landmass. It is also a site of strategic mineral resources, and a key geographic bridge for China's overland pipelines and transport corridors to access energy supplies from Central Asia, Caspian Sea, and potentially Iran, Iraq and Afghanistan.

More importantly, it is a key site of China's nuclear arsenal and China's extensive underground nuclear tunnels are also located around Urumqi - the capital of the Xinjiang Uyghur Autonomous Region -. As such, any instability of Xinjiang and potential jihadists access to China's nuclear arsenal is a red line for Beijing.

It is true that unlike USA, People's republic has been always reluctant to shape countries and take positions especially in the middle east. China for example never made pesky human right criticisms considering that she has to respect choice made by the Arab people, and supports Arab states in exploring their own development paths, the ones suited to their national conditions.

However, there is a revolution ongoing as can be seen in Pentagon recent reports. Obama Administration was indeed stunned as thousands of Chinese troops enter ISIS war. The Kremlin have announced that china are to send 5000 of its most elite military forces into the Levant war zone.

The Siberian tiger special forces as well as night tiger's units were given authorization to be deployed by China's people's congress (NPC) on Sunday, after that china passed its first anti-terrorism law allowing their army to take part in anti-terror missions abroad.

Even tough, China, doesn't seem to have the military capability of the united states and Russia to wage an air and ground war on foreign soil, China wants its part of the enormous business opportunities in the war-torn countries in the Middle east.

Contractors are entering Iraq on a massive scale to undertake reconstruction projects and China, Assad's ally has committed more than 30$ billion to post-war rebuilding in Syria.

Several Arab analysts since 2012 saw this move coming and pressed the gulf states to reassure china and provide additional safeguards in terms of oils. However, the sight of Chinese flags being burned does not contribute to persuading to china to soften its stance.

On October 6, 2011, Secretary Clinton accused China of "standing on the wrong side of history" after vetoing a Western blueprint for Syria at the United Nations Security Council. But from the Chinese perspective, the West does not understand what is at stake for China in the Syrian conflict.

Thus, viewing Syria from Beijing, rather than China being on the "wrong side of history," the West may in fact be on the wrong side of Chinese history.

Russia enters to an infinite quagmire.

US reporters have often been judged to be nostalgic, completely obsessed by Assad's primary ally, Vladimir Putin, and even captive of Cold War mentality. However, this would not be the case if Russia did not take such a part of that conflict. So what is she looking for? what made her sent her soldiers so far from her borders? Would she enter an infinite quagmire?

Apart the fight against terrorism that starts to be the common way to justify any foreign intrusion, it is needless to say that there are probably many geopolitical reasons for that.

Actually, Putin think that he understands well how capitalism works and intends to took advantage from it. But playing with fire, he might end up getting burned.

Right after that intelligence assessments reported that Mr Assad's government might be in trouble, Moscow did whatever it figured had to be done, starting bludgeoning C.I.A.-backed rebel forces with an air campaign that has sent them in the end into retreat.

Invited by Assad Government to intervene unlike the US bombings which had been underway regardless of Syria's approval, attacks by Russian long-range bombers, fighter jets, attack helicopters and cruise missiles allowed the Syrian Army to reverse many of the rebel gains — and seize areas near the Turkish border that many thought the government could never reclaim.

About 600 Russian marines landed in Syria with the mission of protecting the main air base in Latakia; that ground force has grown to about 4,000 throughout Syria, including several hundred special forces members. Airstrikes reached nearly 90 on some days.

What pushed Russia to do so ? First a personal motivation of her commander chief. Putin had wowed to prevent Assad from suffering the same fate as Gaddafi.

Putin blamed himself for letting Gaddafi go, for not playing a strong role behind the scenes at the UN when the Western coalition was lobbying to be allowed to undertake the airstrikes that destroyed the regime. Actually it had been told that Putin had watched a video of Gaddafi's savage death three times, a video that shows him being sodomised with a bayonet.

So even though this implies some fatalities in the blowing of 39 factions which have been fitfully armed and supported by the Central Intelligence Agency, fortifying Assad on Battlefield was considered as the only way to keep him physically alive and politically immovable.

Second is the commercial aspect. Of course, no one can deny that Syria war was as much a mediated weapons and hardware expo as it was a client rescue mission.

The 45 or so fixed-wing aircraft deployed to Bassel al-Assad International Airport in Latakia, now a permanent Russian garrison and airbase on the Mediterranean, ranged from souped-up Soviet models to state-of-the-art killing machines.

Taking part of the bombing of the barracks and weapons depots of the free Syrian army, the Su-34, Russian Air Force's most modern ground attack jet, was showcased as a source of enormous national pride. Several potential buyers like Vietnam, Iraq, Kazakhstan, Turkmenistan, Uzbekistan, Uganda, Nigeria, and Ethiopia are now making the queue.

Same for the new Kalibr missile which has been fired by Russian warships across 900 miles of sea and land, across Iranian and Iraqi airspace. the display became a marquee event for Kremlin-run television, here acting as a multimedia brochure for Rosoboronexport, the Russian state arms dealer.

IHS Jane's, a British defense intelligence firm, calculates that Russia has spent between $5 million and $7.5 million per day on the war in Syria. After 167 days, that comes to anywhere between $668 million and $1.25 billion. The Russian defense budget for 2015 was $50 billion; Rosoboronexport claimed on Dec. 30, 2015, that its arms exports amounted to $15.2 billion, a figure that will likely grow in 2016.;

Last but not least, is the retaining access to the long-time Russian naval base on the Mediterranean Sea.

But at which price?

Putin's Russia enters the quagmire in Syria, for the same reason Bush's America landed in a decade long quagmire in Iraq: Putin apparently thought a few Russian airstrikes in Syria will end the civil war against President Bashar Assad and rout the Islamic State. Unfortunately, the last events may contradict him.

It is true that the dirty war conducted in Ukraine has demonstrated that Putin's tolerance for absorbing plausibly deniable fatalities in murky foreign adventures is much higher than what U.S. spooks intend. But until when ?

As recently as on august, the aircrew of a Russian helicopter shot down in northern Syria met a grisly and macabre end likely sending shockwaves through the Kremlin.

A video showing locals dragging the body of the Russian pilot along the floor - with one man jumping on the deceased - could prove to be Moscow's "Mogadishu moment" and cause a major re-think of the country's motives in the war.

One would think that such animosity toward Russia is limited to ISIS territory, but that would be a wholly false assumption.

June 2015, Abu Muhammad Al-Adnani, one of the Islamic State's senior leaders, declared the existence of a new Wilayat Qawqaz, or Caucasus governorate, and violence increased again as ISIS ordered suicide bombings and murders.

February 2016, local police and federal anti-terrorism special units have reinforced their positions all across Caucasus region, as ISIS-connected terrorist groups have targeted federal highways, attacked and murdered officials, killed tourists—and claimed credit for all these atrocities.

Economically, it is not any better. While the Russian Direct Investment Fund has announced the creation of investment partnerships with the sovereign wealth funds of Saudi Arabia and the United Arab Emirates, the protracted military operation of the Russian army in Syria made the probability of the realization of these plans fall sharply.

These funds were expecting to invest, respectively, $10 billion and $7 billion in projects in Russia. They were considered crucial to provide Russian economy with a new lease on life.

While he was thought strategist, Putin might be just a tactician, and his whole foreign policy might amount to one blunder after another. Obama, already more committed than he wants, would just have to sit back and let Putin defeat himself.

the upcoming disaster will be that Putin starts to be tempted to throw ground troops into the mix, creating the political trap that all Russian analysts foresaw previously for Bush.

To conclude, as said the pragmatic pamphlet "Russia beyond the headlines", the Russian military operation in Syria, in the short term, neither holds any significant losses (expenses) for Russia, nor promises any significant gains. At the same time, in the event of a more serious and long-term involvement in the civil war in Syria, Russia may face significant economic losses.

Russia partnership: An American poker strike.

For those who do not know, we assisted to a policy reversal when US Secretary of State John Kerry travelled to Russia to seek Moscow's cooperation in the war against the ISIS terrorist group in Syria, even as the two countries face worsening relations over the conflicts in Syria and Ukraine as well as NATO's expansion to Russian borders.

Unlike what can be depicted in western newspapers, there has always been a military to military relationship with Russia since the fall of the Soviet Union. After 1991 the US spent billions of dollars to help Russia secure its nuclear weapons complex, including a highly secret joint operation to remove weapons grade uranium from unsecured storage depots in Kazakhstan.

During the American war on Afghanistan, Russia provided overflight rights for US cargo carriers and tankers, as well as access for the flow of weapons, ammunition, food and water the US war machine needed daily.

Russia's military provided intelligence on Osama bin Laden's whereabouts and helped the US negotiate rights to use an airbase in Kyrgyzstan.

And when it comes to tackling Islamic State, Russia and the US have much to offer each other. Many in the IS leadership and rank and troops fought for more than a decade against Russia in the two Chechen wars that began in 1994, Russia knows the ISIS leadership and has insights into its operational techniques, and has much intelligence to share, an intelligence for which US agencies are paying huge sums of cash, from sources within rebel militias. So why the cooperation is not straightforward?

The answer is on the aims pursed and they are totally different. Obama administration didn't take this path persisting on condemning Russia for its support of Assad. A retired senior diplomat who served at the US embassy in Moscow expressed sympathy for Obama's dilemma as the leader of the Western coalition opposed to Russia's aggression against Ukraine: 'Ukraine is a serious issue and Obama has been handling it firmly with sanctions. Last July during a NATO summit, US president has indeed urged leaders of the western military alliance to stand firm against Russia over its "seizure" of the Crimea peninsula from Ukraine.

According to one US official speaking on condition of anonymity, "There are two basic problems that cannot be ignored. One: The Russians' aim in Syria is still either keeping Assad in power or finding some successor who is acceptable to them. ... And two: Putin has proved over and over again, and not just in Syria, that he cannot be trusted to honor any agreement he makes if he decides it's no longer in Russia's interest"

So what is behind the slightest infringement observed this summer? US top diplomat are expecting by sharing its intelligence, to coordinate the air strikes against DAECH and prohibit the Syrian air forces from attacking "moderate" rebels group.

Indeed beyond the minimal coordination that has been held by the past to avoid unintended conflict between their warplanes, information on the location of rebel groups will be now shared to ensure that strikes aimed at terror organizations did not hit American backed groups. In other words, the two sides would trough joint analysis, decide who to target.

Presented as the best chance to limit the fighting that is driving thousands of Syrians, mixed with some trained Islamic State Fighters, into exile in Europe and humanitarian aid from reaching tens of thousands more, as well as preventing a political track, the secretary state hopes getting the US in the same tactical room and to press Moscow to guarantee that Assad's planes will stop bombing.

But the devils are on the details.

First, secretary of state John Kerry refused to list the terms of the agreement. This lack of details makes the deal very suspicions. "The fact no details were announced indicates whatever was agreed was hard to swallow and may be hard to implement. Mr. Kerry conceded probably too much" said Andrew J. Tabler of the Washington Institute for Near East Policy.

John Kerry can emphasize as much as he likes, that the deal is not based on trust but on specific steps that needed to be taken by both sides, the fact remains that Russia is an untrustworthy partner in Syria.

The Syrians and the Russians have routinely undermined previous cease-fires and other measures to spare civilian lives. Several times, the Syrian Army has announced cease-fires, only to conduct military campaigns as around the rebel-held section of Aleppo, leaving about 300,000 people besieged.

"Every time while talking to Assad we have to convince him, give arguments, additional guarantees. ... We can't give him orders, he's on his own soil " Andrei Klimov, deputy chairman of the international committee in Russia's parliament, told Reuters. "US have been saying constantly he's an outcast ... and now they're about to tell Assad, 'You know, please give us a day's advance notice before you want to trash someone with your forces.'"

Second and even worst, the agreement might lead the United States to support or even participate in strikes against groups fighting Mr. Assad as one of the great complications of the Syrian civil war is figuring out which groups should be considered rebels focused on ousting the Assad government — a goal the United States supports — and which groups are aligned with Al Qaeda or the Islamic State.

Undeniably, The Nusra Front has been one of the most effective anti-Assad forces, and American-backed rebel groups often coordinate their activities with its units. The United States has carried out occasional strikes against what have been described as senior Qaeda figures in Syria. But it has refrained from systematic attacks against the Nusra Front, whose ranks are heavily Syrian, including many who left less extreme rebel groups because Nusra was better armed and financed.

In a conclusion, a joint campaign against Al Nusra not only would appear to concede Russia's point, but could also bring American firepower to bear against the strongest anti-Assad military force and a sometime partner of Washington's allies.

Since the beginning of this bilateral negotiation, many officials have expressed concerns. Robert Ford, a former U.S. ambassador to Syria and now a senior fellow at the Middle East Institute think tank in Washington, told Reuters that whether it was Moscow's bad intent or lack of leverage, "it's not clear to me that the Russians can deliver on their side of the deal." Even The top U.S. commander for the fight against the Islamic State of Iraq and Syria (ISIS) said Monday that he is skeptical of any additional military cooperation with Russia in Syria, and that he believes he can get the mission done without it.

And of course, they were right, of course, and it did not take long for their concerns to become a reality.

August, 2016, one month after the deal, Syrian warplanes for the first time targeted Kurdish armed groups that Washington is supporting on the ground and this after that Russians have been informed.

That usual incident, even if it pushes the first military commander to threaten Syria of retaliatory measure, seems to not change Obama administration's strategy in the region, or lack thereof. indeed, Obama doesn't want to be got involved in any skirmishes during the last six months of its presidency.

Does ISIS contribute to preserving US supremacy ?

US: the best safeguard of freedom of expression

Does ISIS contribute to preserving US supremacy ?

Ban of terrorism speech is unconstitutional and contrary to American history.

The great fear after 9/11 was terrorism arriving on American shores via airplanes, the great fear after Paris and San Bernardino is that it will come via the Internet. From the U.N. Security Council to Congress, the last few weeks have seen calls to crack down on incitement of terrorism online: "to erase the screeds of ISIS propagandists, expunge Islamic State sympathizers from Twitter, and pair federal law enforcement officials and Silicon Valley executives in a quest to extirpate violent radicalism from Twitter and YouTube".

However, these calls run counter to a core precept of the unique American approach to safeguarding freedom of expression and struggle against pernicious ideas.

As matter of fact, in the United States, willingness to protect even dangerous speech dates back to Thomas Jefferson, who wrote : "We have nothing to fear from the demoralizing reasonings of some, if others are left free to demonstrate their errors and especially when the law stands ready to punish the first criminal act produced by the false reasoning."

Today, the jurisprudence - arising from the 1969 Supreme Court case Brandenberg v. Ohio- gives the possibility to the Constitution to ban incitement to violence only when it is intentional and when the action it exhorts is both imminent and illegal. Since then, absent any of the three elements — intention, imminence, or lawlessness — a speech cannot be constitutionally forbidden.

Therefore, broad categories of noxious speech — sloganeering at a Ku Klux Klan rally, holocaust denial, or Nazis marching — are constitutionally protected. This status contrasts sharply with much of the rest of the world, where such speech is subject to government prohibitions.

The United States has been steadfast in refusing to subordinate its broad free speech protections to international norms. In 1992, when the Senate ratified the International Covenant on Civil and Political Rights - the world's premier human rights treaty - it spelled out areas where the international protocol would be overridden by the U.S. Constitution. Among the most prominent pertained to Article 20 of the covenant which bans "national, racial or religious hatred that constitutes incitement to discrimination, hostility or violence." Afraid that this provision overrules the First Amendment, the Senate adopted a reservation stating that "Article 20 does not … restrict the right of free speech and association protected by the Constitution and laws of the United States." In short, while most nations — including such liberal societies as Canada, France, and Germany — accept the Article 20 on interdiction of any incitement to "discrimination, hostility or violence," the United States has judged it unconstitutional.

It must be said that in recent years, Washington has vociferously defended its standard, rejecting efforts at the United Nations to invoke Article 20 as grounds for broad proscriptions of what some consider contemporary forms of incitement.

This has certainly been illustrated most recently by the american backing of the legality to depict the Prophet Mohammed. The Obama administration has clearly argued that the efforts to ban depictions of the Prophet Mohammed and other offenses to religious sensibilities infringe basic precepts of free expression.

Free speech advocates, have constantly urged the United States to stick to a firm line against global bans on hate speech, arguing that the answer to inflammatory speech is not suppression, but more speech.

But now the long-standing U.S. refusal to support broad bans on incitement is under pressure. Families of terrorism victims, political candidates, and the White House are all calling for Silicon Valley to join with the government in fighting digital purveyors of terrorism. The rationale is clear: depriving terrorist conspirators of the tools to proselytize, prey on the impressionable, and plan dastardly acts.

Lawmakers are now clamoring for a more aggressive approach. In mid-December, the House of Representatives unanimously passed a bill entitled "Combat Terrorist Use of Social Media Act of 2015," calling for a comprehensive strategy to curb terrorist messaging online.

Earlier last year, the bill's chief sponsor, Rep. Ted Poe (R-Texas), and other lawmakers wrote to the then-CEO of Twitter expressing concern that terrorists "actively use Twitter to disseminate propaganda, drive fundraising, and recruit new members — even posting graphic content depicting the murder of individuals they have captured."

A census by the Brookings Institution calculated that Twitter was home to at least 46,000 accounts maintained by the Islamic State, many of which will be shut off if the new standard is enforced.

If online companies block this speech voluntarily under their own private content restrictions — rather than submitting to official dictates of censorship — the long-held American fight against large government bans of incitement would have not been vain. US ethics would remain technically intact.

In front of the world, US preserves its ethics and spread its sights.

Several critics are coming from outside US lobbying officials to stop ISIS access to internet and especially from social media. US has long been stymied by militants' ability to use the internet as a vehicle for inspiring so called lone wolf attackers in western nations, radicalized after reading propaganda easily available online like Farouk, San Bernardino's striker.

But looking to it carefully, that is not so easy: governmental cyber teams need to be careful about disrupting the Internet to ensure that attacks don't also affect civilian networks or systems needed for critical infrastructure and other public necessities. Moreover, the military cyber fight is limited by concerns within the intelligence agencies that blocking the group internet access could hurt intelligence gathering. There is a need of creative options that would allow the US to impact ISIS without diminishing the indications or warning intelligences officers can glean about what the group though the internet.

Setting out of this premise and noting that 'standing still is not an option', Obama administration started working out on a dual policy based on a push of private companies to do the ban job on the one hand and setting up a worldwide propaganda against ISIS on the other hand.

In order to not alter the American reputation in terms of freedom of expression, the actions conducted by the American firms would have to be of course in line with the ethics highest standards. Same applies to the propaganda that should be spread from the Muslim countries under US supervision.

Tech firms face dilemma between willingness to censor and the guarantee of integrity.

First illustration of this dual strategy came from the white House itself. Call it the T-Team. The Obama administration brought together some of biggest names in tech to tackle ISIS online.

Executives from Apple, Twitter, Snapchat, Facebook, and MTV met at the Justice Department to discuss a new project nicknamed "Madison Valleywood," a combination of slang industry names, seen as a big part of the president's legacy.

Indeed In front of government disability to ban social media, there is no other way than to line up tech firms: Facebook and Twitter asserted deleting aggressively and mercilessly large   amounts of content and to ban those who post it.

Actually, Twitter began taking a more aggressive approach after videos and images of journalist James Foley's beheading spread on social media. Increased measures to ensure ISIS does not saturate its airwaves with propaganda, led to the suspension of more than 125 00 accounts in the last several months. "The good news is that this limits the reach of their propaganda and recruiting, and makes it harder for ISIS to accomplish its goals online," Berger says.

Facebook CEO, Mark Zuckerberg, also doubled down on his initial commitment to utilize his network to prevent terrorists from spreading their message online. he said earlier that: "Facebook feel like, it has a pretty big reasonability running this big networking community to help prevent the terrorism and different kinds of attacks". "Posts and blocked accounts had been removed in such a way that ISIS-related newsletters, videos, and photos don't seem to crop up as much as elsewhere on the web", says Steve Stalinsky, executive director of Middle East Media Research. "Of all the companies, they're the leader and the best at removing content," he says.

However, these efforts may not be sufficient, indeed ISIS is threatening to take down Facebook and twitter over their effort to prevent the terrorists from utilizing social media. In ISIS video, we can read: "To Mark and Jack, Founders of Facebook and twitter, you announce daily that you spend many of our accounts. and to you, we say: Is that all you can do? You are not in our league. If you close one account, we make 10 in return". This is what it's all about.

In fact, the issue lies in the global nature of social media. First, many of those banned simply open a new account and continue posting their hatred. Second the reliance upon self-policing by users to identify objectionable content.

Indeed, the two platforms are global communities. Being engaged in a constant process of determining community norms as the use of the platforms evolves, a blanket policy of banning anything that might be seen as inciting violence could lead to questions of censorship, because one person's hateful propaganda could be another's free speech.

Several analysts tried so far to address this problem by censoring a certain batch of wording but again messages of resistance that are sinister when posted in the name of the Islamic State may read far more benignly when posted by, for example, radical climate change activists or protesters against Russia President Vladimir Putin. Social media purposefully divorces content from context, forcing readers to discern meaning and intent by drawing on knowledge and understanding that they must aggregate on their own. So while a court may be able to weigh considerations of context carefully and objectively, a young analyst assessing thousands of posts a day and hoping to help stave off further government intrusion into the prerogatives of Silicon Valley seems bound to rely on shorthand involving preconceptions and probably also prejudices.

This without even mentioning that in the rush to expunge terrorism, legitimate voices, ideas, and perspectives might also be suppressed, potentially on suspect grounds relating to religion or national origin.

No one can deny that companies like Facebook and Twitter aren't taking this seriously. But it's not as simple as you might think.

Indeed, borderline questions will inevitably arise with respect to speech that has historically been protected, potentially endless questions, and it is not even clear who will answer them — intelligence analysts, judges, or "junior staff snacking on free food in a Menlo Park conference room". (Menlo park is home to Facebook Headquarters).

For sure, the collaboration called between Washington and Silicon Valley would raise thornier suspicions about who will really decide what speech is off-limits and whether and how they can be held accountable.

When it comes to content itself, the Brandenburg case is relevant. Ideological entreaties, glorifications of martyrs, and celebrations of terrorist acts — however repugnant — are not themselves incitement to violence. They can be monitored, flagged, and even taken down by private parties but not censored under U.S. law.

Besides all that, while there is plenty of room to argue about cause and effect, there is no proof that prohibiting hate speech prevents hate crimes, as an example, fourteen European countries have legally prohibited Holocaust denial (unconstitutional in the United States), and yet anti-Semitism is nonetheless on the rise throughout most of Europe. It is plausible that bad speech may encourage bad acts but also that banning such speech may only strengthen the speaker's determination to get the message out, in deeds if not words.

Moreover, the standards set in the United States will influence the approaches of governments around the world, establishing precedents that their citizens will be forced to live with. Whether it's China's Tibetans, Turkey's PKK, since 9/11 many governments have found it useful to brand their domestic antagonists "terrorists" in order to legitimize repressive tactics. China already passed a harsh new counterterrorism law, invoking global fears of online recruitment and incitement as justification for a measure that provides for broad powers of surveillance and censorship.

In conclusion, categories of speech that do not qualify as incitement — such as terrorist recruitment activity — cannot be banned. At the end, this is to the greater good, because their criminalization would lead America down a slippery slope.

For what it is worth, Australia has ventured into that slope and apparently failed. Islamic leaders argued in 2014 that the definition of incitement under that country's law could criminalize preaching from the Quran as well as backing factions opposed to the rule of Syrian President Bashar al-Assad. The Islamic Council of Victoria has even argued that the proposed counterterrorism measure "could see to it that there are no voices of disagreement or debate on the subject for fear of prosecution."

A Lack of credibility of US propaganda pushes America to outsource it.

Meanwhile legislators and judges were working to consider other ways to target and prohibit hate speeches, talks have started between the tech firms and counterintelligence officials about the only alternative remaining: the "counter-narratives and optimistic messaging,"

Notable was by the way Apple's appearance at the meeting in light of its recent stance in favor of user privacy over government interference.

Unfortunately, glimmers of hope have quickly been extinguished. A review by outside experts revealed several doubts on the U.S. government's ability to serve as a credible voice against the terrorist group's propaganda, doubts that pushed the State Department to consider scaling back its direct involvement in online campaigns to discredit the Islamic State.

The findings which has been conducted by marketing experts from Silicon Valley and New York, have added to the uncertainty surrounding a State Department's program that also faced another management shake-up with the departure of its second director in less than a year, a departure which has brought new tumult to a unit already associated with frequent changes of strategy and personnel.

The figures were actually clear and irrevocable: none of the participants speak Arabic, were knowledgeable about terrorist groups or had security clearances that would enable them to evaluate classified work. "They were largely on the marketing and branding side — looking at ISIL and the U.S. governments as brands," said a U.S. official familiar with the review. There was no added value in the work done by teams of analysts and contractors who posted hundreds of messages and videos each month in Arabic, English and other languages — all under the State Department seal.

Even though, US propaganda was trending upward mounting campaigns on Twitter, Facebook, sowing doubt among those who may join ISIS over the past two years, it was obvious that a radical change of course was needed. A change of strategy mainly justified by the constant adaptations by the Islamic State seeking to put pressure on the U.S. government to keep pace. "They learn from their mistakes. They change and adapt to the digital battlefield," said the Secretary of State for Public Diplomacy and Public Affairs, Richard Stengel. As a result, "the State Department program "has to be equally creative and innovative."

According to same report, new policy should involve more partnership with credible voices as other governments and third parties. There is a need to set up messaging centers overseas with the expectation that their postings would have greater credibility and impact than those coming from the U.S. government.

An advice taken seriously as centers in the United Arab Emirates and Malaysia became operational this year while others are planned in Jordan and Nigeria.

The review also backed ideas that have languished for lack of funding at the State Department, including a plan to create counter-radicalization "SWAT" teams that could be deployed to cities in Europe and elsewhere where officials see spikes in Islamic State recruitment.

Direct-messaging operation could be downsized and focused more narrowly on themes such as the campaign centered on Islamic State defectors that was launched this year.

Hussain, the American Muslim with close ties to the White House, arrived at the State Department this year with a mandate to end what critics called "tweeting at terrorists." He replaced Alberto M. Fernandez, who had pushed the center to take a more combative approach online with barbed exchanges on Twitter and with videos that mocked the Islamic State, often by using footage of its atrocities.

A smart use of censorship.

Though, several efforts have been made by the federal state to show its attachment to the first amendment, it seems that a smart and tricky use of censorship has been now developed for many years .

Indeed, while the Supreme Court prohibit any form of banning, states are busy crafting censorship laws at home. At least thirteen states have passed legislation since 1995. This year, New Mexico has already passed a draconian censorship law, and bills are pending in 10 other states.

these state bills raise serious free speech concerns. Aimed at the beginning to keep adult materials away from minors, laws end up reducing all online content preventing both adults and teenagers from getting access to valuable speech like sex education materials, abuse recovery discussions, and speech about lesbian and gay issues.

These state laws pose a cumulative threat to online speech because every online user must comply with every state law -- or risk prosecution if their speech is accessed in a state that makes it illegal. Actually, the draconian effect of state censorship bills doesn't stop at state borders. A message you post on the Internet today in New York City could travel the fifty states and the globe by tomorrow. You'd better be careful that the message isn't "indecent" in Oklahoma, "annoying" in Connecticut, or "vulgar" in Georgia.

Another mean to deny non-comfortable speech is the practice of heavy political pressure.

While for ISIS such pressure came from Anonymous claiming that Silicon Valley firms as "cloud Fare" were helping ISIS bolster speeding up and improving their online security, cutting WikiLeaks got a large support from both democrats and republicans.

Indeed, the same officials that brought support to the Californian firm's objection to exercise tight control about what can be served in its servers, massively applaud Amazon's removal of WikiLeaks.

Lieberman, chairman of the Senate's committee on homeland security, said: "[Amazon's] decision to cut off WikiLeaks now is the right decision and should set the standard for other companies WikiLeaks is using to distribute its illegally seized material. I call on any other company or organization that is hosting WikiLeaks to immediately terminate its relationship with them."

Furthermore, The US government does not flinch to use the extraterritoriality of its judicial power. Last example up to date, the establishment of a treasury department blacklist. To be part of the list has for consequence to have all domain related to you disabled.

That was the case for Steve Marshall an English travel agent that sells trips to Cuba. Accused to be a generator of resources that the Cuban regime would late uses to oppress its people, he saw not less than 80 of his websites appear as 'not working anymore'.

As many large domain name registrars are based in the United States, Treasury's Office of Foreign Assets Control, has control over a great deal of speech. Not even a judge is required for the U.S. government to censor online materials of Web sites owned by a British national operating via a Spanish travel agency.

Las but not least, is the use of the economic arm. Being the world's largest advertising agency, google AdSense justifies its decision to disable some websites by the violation of its content policies.

This has earned the media giant to be the target of several protesters which accused him to be an arm of the US state department.

To conclude, the future of censorship is even more bright, as evidenced anew the refusal of the Federal Communications Commission (FCC) head to appear before the people's representatives in Congress.

Tom wheeler, FCC chairman, which is ready to issue a new rule for the internet which is misnamed "Net neutrality", seems not to be in position to ensure the freedom of speech.

For those who doesn't know, Net neutrality is the principle that Internet service providers should give consumers access to all legal content and applications on an equal basis, without favoring or blocking some sources. It also prohibits Internet service providers (ISPs) from charging content providers for speedier delivery of their content on "fast lanes" or deliberately slowing the content from content providers that may compete with ISPs.

I let you imagine what can be done with such rules if they are turned in someone's favor.

Does ISIS contribute to preserving US supremacy ?

Well instrumented, ISIS fight is a differentiation element

Does ISIS contribute to preserving US supremacy ?

A game of cat and mouse; the white house and Congress.

President Obama achieved last year a great master stroke in his fight against congress. The authorization to use military forces (AUMF) raised by him, confronted congressman with a sort of cornelian dilemma.

The Republican majority of the congress which always wants to reclaim its authority, has had either to vote for a new AUMF, endorse Obama and send a message of resolve , or vote against which should certainly delight the defence lobby but highlight their inaction.

Indeed, since the beginning of the military campaign against ISIL last summer, the administration has claimed that the AUMF adopted after the attacks of 9/11 to authorize war against al Qaeda and the Taliban somehow authorizes this new war fourteen years later against a new enemy in different countries.

Actually, the proposed authorization for use of military force gives approval for open-ended and geographically limitless military operations. Its vague wording leaves the door open to the use of ground troops, which the administration has previously vowed to avoid, but does nothing to repeal the sweeping 2001 AUMF.

However with a limitation of three years and a prohibition against "enduring offensive ground combat operations (whatever that means), I let you imagine the outcry if the future republican president deviated military from President Obama's current course of action. Would the introduction on the ground of a brigade combat team lead to calls for impeachment? If ISIS proves resilient in the face of mandate limited war (as would be likely) would US face a national debate over mandatory withdrawal and retrieval?

Clearly, President Obama wants the dog and the pony show of getting an AUMF that ties his hands so he can either blame congress or hamstring his successor in office.

In reality, Obama, being non belligerent, sees in this new AUMF the only way to cabin future presidential war-making power. Indeed, by claiming authority under the 2001 AUMF, presidents have had military force deployed in Afghanistan, Pakistan, Arabian Peninsula, Yemen against Al Qaeda, in Somalia against members of al Shabaab and who knows where else.

Whatever the merits of some readings of the 2001 AUMF, to now extend it to the war against ISIL is senseless. The U.S. is now engaged in a new fight against a new enemy in different countries, an enemy that is in competition and sometimes actual conflict with al Qaeda. If the 2001 AUMF is deemed to authorize this war, it is hard to imagine any circumstances where it could not be argued to apply.

Congress ended up by rejecting Obama's AUMF request and instead gave him what he needed. Through this move , Republican senators were expecting to show to American people that either the democrats have finally filibustered it or the president himself refused to fight.

Meanwhile on the Democrat side, congressmen were expressing worries claiming that the draft AUMF sent by the president would constitute a blank check for war extending far beyond the current operations in Iraq and Syria. According to them, the devastating and costly wars in Iraq and Afghanistan have taught them that when they give military authority to the executive, it should not be a blank check. But in reality, adopting a new AUMF for the war against IS won't be a blank check for war; doing nothing, failing to vote on a new AUMF, will de-facto be the blank check.

In conclusion, thanks to a specific wording of this AUMF, congress is left on the side-lines meanwhile the president continues to claim reliance on the 2001 AUMF as his wish.

Orlando shooting raises a critical juncture of the second amendment.

Considered as the deadliest terrorist attack on US soil since 9/11, Orlando shooting revealed once again how instrumented the ISIS fight is for ideological aims.

To provide some history: Omar Mateen opened fire early July in a packed Orlando Nightclub, killing fifty (50) people and wounding fifty three (53) more. Even though the target -gay bar- as well as the timing -Islamic holy month- argue for direct ties between Mateen and ISIS, officials argue it remains unclear if the planning and execution of the attack were directly linked to foreign terrorist groups

Indeed despite all these suspicious elements, News networks reported that the terrorist pledged allegiance to ISIS just few moments before the shooting and that ISIS claimed responsibility only the day after without offering any proof of advance knowledge.

However, what has been strongly highlighted is the relatively easy access to powerful weapons in the united states, a longstanding concern of US counterterrorism.

Actually besides the Orlando one, there have been a string of deadly Islamic terrorist attacks involving firearms including the killing of five members of US military in July 2015 as well as in San Bernardino last December.

Same warning bell for President Obama which even though he made no new specific calls for stricter gun laws, lamented "how easy it is" for people to get their hands on weapons.

For the president, the hastily arranged remarks were the latest in what's become a tragically familiar routine. Since he took office in 2009, Obama has appeared before cameras more than a dozen times following mass shootings. He issued several written statements after many others imploring the nation to finally get serious about stemming gun violence.

Acting as multiplier opinion, Senator Dick Durbin and Governor Andrew Cuomo addressed the attack as a "horrific reminder for lawmakers about the need for stricter gun control. For the policymakers, congress "have the power to act, and he must, if congress does not act, he would be complicit in the next killing"

Though, such trickery does not intend to stop up to the race for the White House.

Meanwhile Donald Trump, the presumptive Republican presidential nominee, was citing the mass shooting to advance his argument that legal and illegal immigration are endangering U.S. security, Clinton took this opportunity to emphasize her strong bonds with the LGBT community as well as her fight for gun control: "to the LGBT community: Please know that you have millions of allies across our country. I am one of them. This tragedy it reminds us once more that weapons of war have no place on our streets" Clinton said.

By contrast, among those who would like to linger over the terrorist issue, the attack is presented mainly as a sign of weakness coming from the terror group.

Indeed, since the beginning of Ramadan, the terror group requests from its sympathizers to stay home and kill anybody anyhow anywhere. "The smallest action you do in the heart of their land is dearer to us than the largest action by us, and more effective and more damaging to them" ISIS spokesman said.

Such call was presented as a part of an all-out campaign revenge waged by ISIS as it loses both territory in Middle East and notoriety in western countries. Actually, the attack came a time when there were some signs ISIS was losing its appeal in united states. Confronted to a sharp drop in the number of Americans sympathizers (from six (6) new per month in 2015 to just one (1) in 2016), ISIS is inventing theological precepts to suit their purposes as the non-sense tenfold reward in paradise for carrying out attacks during Ramadan.

Pentagon, White house: a sneaky cooperation.

Since the rise of ISIS, perspectives coming from pentagon and white house are to say the least not inline, if not contradictory. This difference in approach let to a sneak cooperation.

Since the beginning, Obama's administration approach was seen by the military officers as simply as fixation on Assad's primary ally, Vladimir Putin. In their view, the White house is captive to Cold War thinking about Russia and China, and doesn't care much of the spread of terrorism in and beyond Syria.

'Our policy of arming the opposition to Assad was unsuccessful and actually having a negative impact,' the former Joint Chiefs of staff (JCS) adviser said. 'The Joint Chiefs believed that Assad should not be replaced by fundamentalists.

Tired to send a constant stream of classified warnings to the civilian leadership without results, General Michael Flynn, according to a controversy article by Seymour Hersh, decided "to take steps against the extremists without going through political channels, by providing US intelligence to the militaries of other nations, on the understanding that it would be passed on to the Syrian army and used against the common enemy, Jabhat al-Nusra and Islamic State."

Germany, Israel and Russia were indeed in contact with the Syrian army, and able to exercise some influence over Assad's decisions – it was through them that US intelligence might be shared. Each one driven by its own reasons, they all thought that sharing US assessments could prove productive results. It was clear that Assad needed better tactical intelligence and operational advice.

This could have continued for a while, if general Flynn, had not insisted on telling the truth about Syria, and doing so incurred the wrath of the White House.

Former Pentagon chief Chuck Hagel has caught by the same squeeze too. Coming out recently against the White House matters, everyone knew at that time that President Obama and him did not see eye-to-eye on how to prosecute the war against the Islamic State, Hagel simply needed to go. White House had purely lost faith in Hagel's ability to lead.

The same applies for previous secretaries of state Gates and Panetta. Both have served for President Obama and both have affirmed that "the suspicion and distrust of senior military officers by senior White House officials — including the president and vice president — had become a big problem for them as they spent all their time trying to manage the relationship between the commander in chief and his military leaders." According to them, President Obama "relies on the logic of a law professor rather than the passion of a leader."

It is only recently that relations have been improved. It must be said that the nomination of Ashton Carter as secretary of state, has been also an essential key to this as he has restored the communications bridge between the administration, the Pentagon, and Central Command.

Carter was not the administration's first choice, and got some knocks within the Pentagon for keeping policymaking to a very small group of his closest advisers, but military and intelligence officials have all recognized at the end that he had bridged the trust-and-comprehension gulf between the administration and military leaders.

"Carter plays a more active role than his predecessor. He's made himself quite prominent in the ISIS fight," said one senior military official. "He's a detail guy and that has been well received. "

There's more clarity between Washington and the outstations."

GOP presidential primaries have shown that two schools of thought emerge and will likely dispute.

Following the San-Bernardino terrorist attack as well as the Orlando one, the 2016 presidential campaign just became a foreign policy election.

However, listening to all presidential campaign speeches, it remains unclear how many of the candidates for the major election would specifically shift US military strategy against ISIS.

No Republican wants to admit it, but their ISIS strategies are largely the same as Obama's apart from a bit of isolationism.

All republicans, all along the primaries, agreed that ISIS had emerged largely if not solely due to the weakness of one Barack Obama, indeed they are all expecting to clean up the mess left by the current administration.

However, none of these candidate, not even the newly elected one, had any remotely plausible ideas on how to defeat ISIS, or prevent terrorist attacks on American soil, beyond what Obama was already doing—except doing it louder, or with a scarier scowl, or maybe doing more of it.

During 2016 December debate between republican candidates, 90 minutes of which focused on ISIS and terrorism, every one of the runners on stage made some version of this argument:

- Obama's ISIS strategy is failing because Obama is personally weak or dishonest.
- My ISIS strategy is better because I am stronger and tougher.
- My strategy differs from Obama's because I will do the exact same things but with more strength and toughness.

This led the candidates to focus overwhelmingly on differences of personality and temperament, which they argued, implausibly, make all the difference.

But the candidates focused on these personality differences because it's all they have. There are few real policy differences to talk about, so all they can do is argue that they are personally tougher and stronger in ways that will somehow prove decisive.

This promotion of the identity and the personality falls within the readiness to sign up in US foreign policy's cleavages: isolationist against interventionist, idealist in front of realist, unilateral against multilateral.

Indeed, there has always been two diverging schools of thought inside the GOP: one willing to restore the preponderance of the country and other one less hawkish turned forward to an internationalism pragmatism.

Marco Rubio, the defeated candidate of the GOP establishment, represents quite well the first school. Indeed, according to Florida Senator, the fact that ISIS had the ambitions and capabilities to execute large-scale attacks against the West and harm Americans at home, largely justifies the dispatch of a larger number of Americans troops on the ground, working with local tribes. "If America, does not make this our fight, the west will not win it, in this clash of civilization, either we win or they win" he said.

Interventionist school of thought, had in mind to establish a coordinate political military strategy which can be summarized briefly by : first confront ISIL in Iraq and Syria then stop the spread of the terror group across the middle east and finally protect the homeland.

To do so, it was expecting to build a multinational coalition of countries willing to send troops with embedded US forces and US logistical and intelligence support to aid local fighters on the ground in destroying ISIS's safe heavens as well as expand airstrikes deploying forward air controllers to call in air support.

However, the plan of former GOP favorite candidate was not limited to a military front but also to the politic and economic ones, Florida senator would have

- Countered ISIS recruitment and propaganda by broadcasting US victories, showing the world that ISIS is not invincible;
- Work with Baghdad to increase Sunni inclusion and autonomy for the provinces;
- Push back against Iranian influence in Iraq, which stokes further conflict;
- Coordinate with regional allies to plan for Assad's fall;
- Advocate on Behalf of and protect ethnic and religious minorities throughout the region.
- Enhance military and diplomatic efforts to prevent ISIS from further entrenching itself in Afghanistan as well as take action to ensure ISIS does not spread to countries like Jordan;
- Target ISIS's financial reserves with sanctions and asset freezes and continue to undermine its attempts to exploit sources.
- Engage in global ideological pushback by exposing ISIS's war crimes and sex trafficking and recruiting disaffected former members to tell their stories.

Meanwhile, Donald Trump, the freshly elected president, which is an advocate of pragmatism in the campaign, was not sharing such interventionism ideals.

Indeed, behind its crass remarks on US foreign policy, Donald Trump's proposal to act in America own interest, without vain ambitions and within international institutions is in reality an idea long while endorsed by many republicans as strange as this might sound.

Trump, the troublemaker, was promoting during his campaign a supporting role away from regional conflict that cost a lot and confined to a fight against ISIL rather than the departure of the Syrian dictator.

U.S. foreign policy would start moving away from ruinously expensive and ultimately pointless interventionist actions overseas. Other nations would be expected to step up and take greater responsibility for their own protection.

Trump literally pointed out that "the wealth of American middle class has been ripped from their homes and then redistributed all across the world." he planned to pull in American horns and withdraw the US from the world.

he "promised" that there would be major changes in the way the U.S. has approached global issues since the end of the Second World War.

In short, with trump present, there would be major changes in the way the U.S. has approached global issues since the end of the Second World War.

Once elected, Trump moves from isolationist to interventionist without necessarily meeting its detractors expectations.

Behind this shift, Two main reasons stand out.

Firstly, the establishment's determination to remain a major player in this part of the world: Indeed, with the United States absent in Syria, Russia participated in the army on the side of the Syrian leader Bashar al- Assad and left Washington outside the power game dominated by Moscow and Assad-ally Iran. He also left the US without influence in the peace talks sponsored by Vladimir Putin in Russia.

Secondly, trump advisors see in the military campaign against ISIS, a great opportunity to rebuild its presidential image.

Unlike some polemical topics such as Obama care or trade exchange, the fight against terrorism will receive a broad consensus, regardless of political stripes and allegiances to national unity.

Yet again, it's one thing to decide you want to win and it's quite another getting it! Especially in view of Trump first arbitrations

Indeed, one week after that he proposed shifting billions from the State Department to the Pentagon, two of the top U.S. generals in the Middle East and Africa say they need diplomatic help.

As said by many top war commanders for many years about fighting terrorism, "success requires more than a quick military campaign. It is only through a combination of capabilities that we will achieve and sustain our strongest deterrence posture."

According to them, If newly elected President wants to "start winning wars again," he would do well to fund the State Department's non-military work in the Middle East and Africa and plan for long-term political solutions.

a concern shared even among GOP, as demonstrated in republican senator Lindsey Graham declaration "Any budget that we pass that guts the State Department, we'll never win this war. In fact, ISIL will be celebrating"

Incidentally, several analysts are saying that this subject is beyond the scope of the fight against ISIS. These proposed cuts are dangerous as they could help bring about dueling U.S. foreign policies—one made by generals and another made by diplomats.

The cuts alone won't muddle America's voice in the world. But they could tip a long-running debate over the role of civilian agencies in determining U.S. foreign policy.

Very quickly, the U.S. government faces the potential that generals will drive foreign policy.

Syrian refugees, a boon for far fight groups

The latest terror attacks occurred in western Europe, apart forcing trump to take the gloves off against ISIS, pushed the president to focus on protecting the homeland.

This national security concern was largely instrumented by Donald trump looking to "MAKE AMERICA SAFE AGAIN". He urged and tried through the Muslim ban act to stop the existing massive refugee inflows into the united states under President Obama as there's no way to screen these refugees in order to accurately find out who they are or where they come from. Trump only wanted to admit individuals into who will support America values and love Americans

In reality, welcoming Syrian refugees poses virtually zero threat to national security. The current vetting method contains a nine-step investigation full of background checks, data collection, investigations by the FBI and State Department, and fingerprinting screened against enormous biometric databases of watch-list information and records captured in Iraq. Syrian cases are also the most strictly monitored, so only the strongest candidates for resettlement (less than one percent of the refugee population) are able to pass even step one of the nine-step process. It would be unreasonable for anyone in the Republican Party to say that the current vetting process makes America unsafe.

ISIS: A crisis which will last.

Does ISIS contribute to preserving US supremacy ?

An enemy much tougher than thought.

More than once the Pentagon has proved to be overly optimistic about its campaign against ISIS only to discover it is confronting an adaptable group, tempering with some officials' willingness to call recent ISIS losses a win.

Indeed, the more the militaries learn about ISIS, the longer and harder they think this fight will be. ISIS turned out to be innovative, agile, and resilient. According to Elton, the deputy commanding general for the top U.S. military counterterrorist unit, ISIS is "ready to fail multiple times, ready to accept tremendous losses to advance their cause."

ISIS fighters quickly adapt their organization and their technologies, their tactics, techniques and procedures, their weapons, to take advantage of coalition constraints and limitations "They hide in populated urban areas, communicate with leading edge encryption, executive effective mission command, and they develop affordable but lethal weapons, particularly explosives made from commercially available materials. While improvise armor and working on chemical and biological weapons"

Even though the prevailing view is that the group is in trouble, weakened by both the coalition attacks and the departure of extensive personnel, there is a bunch of analysts that argue that, while weaker, ISIS is strategically saving its forces to protect its Iraqi and Syrian capitals, Mosul and Raqqa, and the cities that support those capitals.

Looking how quick was the recent regain of the central Syrian cities, it seems that the terror group just retreated. There were by the way early indications that ISIS forces fled toward hotly contested but more strategic cities.

Apart Raqqa and Mosul, which are the main capitals of the Islamic state in Iraq and Syria, they are much more valuable cities to protect than the one's lost. Cities like Homs are key potential revenue sources. And Aleppo is a critical route between the self-proclaimed caliphate and the West.

Indeed, one of the major lesson ISIS gained from the battle for the northern city of Kobane was not to expend resources in conventional clashes unless they are critical to the group's survival. The regain of the city of Kobane by Kurdish forces, was the last major battle ISIS launched and losses have been tremendous.

Even though not widespread, this view is shared by James Clapper, National intelligence director. "They've lost a lot of territory," he said. "We're killing a lot of their fighters. We will retake Mosul, but it will take a long time and be very messy. I don't see that happening in this administration. "

In addition of Mossul not retaken this year, clapper is concerned that problem of terrorism will persist long after they are defeated in Iraq and Syria and that US cannot fix it.

According to him, "The fundamental issues they have — the large population bulge of disaffected young males, ungoverned spaces, economic challenges and the availability of weapons — won't go away for a long time".

It looks like that The president, who wanted to be known as the commander in chief who decimated al Qaeda, is going down in history as having ceded the battlefield to al Qaeda's successor, ISIS.

Eagerness to kill VS willingness to die.

Since deadliest attacks on 9/11, the United States is engaged in a very costly, long and unsuccessful war against a shadowy enemy that for sure will not be defeated for decades to come.

Partly to not say mainly, Barack Obama was elected president to bind up the nation's wounds and withdraw its troops. Yet the enemy, in the form of the Islamic State, remains.

The president has so far struggled to come by a talk that distinguishes between force, which most Americans want, and war which they don't. He has therefore promised, vowed, pledged that, come what may, there will not be "boots on the ground."

But what "boots on the grounds" means? initially and before been weaponized by the presidential campaign, it served as a self-evident expression signifying that soldiers were present in a combat setting.

Now it has degenerated into a figure of speech, an arbitrary boundary between "war" and "not war." "Boots on the ground" signifies war; the president has promised no more war; ergo, there are no boots on the ground. Drones are a far better alternative, which do not require boots in the sky, even less on the ground.

In reality, such features are not new. Tired of post-cold war conflicts, American desperation has forced Clinton at that time to end the fighting in Bosnia in 1995 through air power alone. Indeed the death of 18 Army Rangers in first cold war conflict in Somalia, has turned Americans decisively against military involvement in the subsequent ones.

For those who think that such reluctance is typical to democrats, it is worthy to not that even republicans, always eager to see their bellicosity brandish, have promised those boots on the ground before putting them on someone else's feet. Actually, Ted Cruz, the candidate of conservatism, has appealed several times "the United States to carpet-bomb ISIS, but of course someone else would have to do the fighting. "Kurdish pesh merga, for example would be critical boots on the ground."

However, Americans do not feel that way right now about the terror group, and another ISIS-inspired killing like the Orlando attack might quickly change that.

In reality, they would like to bomb 'shit out' of them but are not ready to bear the consequences of such war. Rarely has the discrepancy been so great between their eagerness to kill and their willingness to die.

Actually, this new penchant for war without boots feeds a dangerous delusion. even if endorsed by many of Obama's Republican rivals, it is misleading to think that United States can smash its foes in the Middle East at the same time as it withdraws from the region and, in fact, from much of the world.

US supremacy relies indeed on the presence of its soldiers all around the world as well as their ability to treat quickly all the conflicts.

With the presidential elections nearing, many Americans believes in the coming of providential man, however unsure that act would be sufficient. Indeed, the ISIS problem is more complex than thought.

Despite the impression given by the different president speeches, foreign policy is not shaped by the gut instincts of the commander in chief but rather by a vast network of foreign policy professionals and institutions. Even if a new president comes in planning to change everything, he or she typically ends up largely maintaining the status quo. Actually, personalizing foreign policy to the president is just a stratagem used by newspaper to make it easier to follow.

Indeed American foreign policy, with some meaningful exceptions, tends to be pretty consistent across administrations. That's especially true when it comes to big and difficult problems like ISIS, and when it comes to complicated inter-agency strategies.

Furthermore, Americans have a sense that ISIS emerged at least in part due to American failures, failures coming from both democrats than republicans

Indeed while some of those failures predated Obama, especially the US invasion of Iraq, others occurred under his presidential watch.

Bibliography

1. <u>ISIS, from an outcome to an asset</u>

- Unfolding the Future of the Long War, Motivations, Prospects, and Implications for the U.S. Army, RAND Corp Report, 2008

- War among terrorists : Al Qaeda declares War against ISIS (URL : http://www.elitereaders.com/al-qaeda-declares-war-against-isis/).

- ISIS and Al-Qaeda go to war with one another in western Syria (URL : https://www.almasdarnews.com/article/jihadist-heavyweight-matchup-isis-al-qaeda-begins-western-syria/).

-Al Qaeda Turns to Syria, With a Plan to Challenge ISIS (URL : http://www.nytimes.com/2016/05/16/world/middleeast/al-qaeda-turns-to-syria-with-a-plan-to-challenge-isis.html?_r=1).

-Comparing Al Qaeda and ISIS: Different goals, different targets (URL : https://www.brookings.edu/testimonies/comparing-al-qaeda-and-isis-different-goals-different-targets/).

- We're getting to know just how different ISIS is from al Qaeda (URL: http://uk.businessinsider.com/difference-between-isis-and-al-qaeda-2015-5?r=US&IR=T).

- America's Allies Are Funding ISIS (URL: http://www.thedailybeast.com/articles/2014/06/14/america-s-allies-are-funding-isis.html).

- Secret pentagon report reveals us "created" ISIS as a "tool" to overthrow Syria's president Assad (URL : http://www.infowars.com/ secret-pentagon-report-reveals-us-created-isis-as-a-tool-to-overthrow-syrias-president-assad/).

- Iraqi PM Can't Please Anyone, How Can He Save the Country? (URL : http://www.niqash.org/en/articles/politics/5150/).

- 13 years Later, Iraq passes de-Baathification Law (URL : http://www.iraq-businessnews.com/2016/08/10/13-years-later-iraq-passes-de-baathification-law/4/).

- Turkey's secret pact with Islamic State exposed by operative behind wave of ISIS attacks (URL : https://medium.com/insurge-intelligence/ turkeys-secret-pact-with-islamic-state-exposed-by-operative-behind-wave-of-isis-attacks-6b35d1d29e18#.x688n8im5).

2. Do US really want ISIS to be defeated?

- Obama Takes the Gloves Off Against ISIS at Last (URL : http://www.thedailybeast.com/articles/2016/01/28/obama-takes-the-gloves-off-against-isis-at-last.html).

- How Special-Ops Is Taking ISIS Out (URL : http://www.thedailybeast.com/articles/2016/05/28/the-gloves-finally-come-off-in-the-isis-war.html).

- Intel chiefs: Saudi, UAE ground troops unlikely to help against ISIS (URL : http://thehill.com/policy/defense/268758-intel-chiefs-saudi-uae-offers-of-ground-troops-against-isis-welcome-unlikely).

- This is the Pentagon's new strategy to defeat ISIS (URL : http://www.militarytimes.com/story/military/war-on-is/2016 /01/14/ pentagon-strategy-islamic-state-iraq-syria/78269180/).

- Military developing plans to move troops closer to front lines in Iraq (URL : http://thehill.com/policy/defense/272660-military-developing-plans-to-move-troops-closer-to-the-front-lines-in-iraq).

- ISIS loses 45 percent of territory in Iraq, 20 percent in Syria (URL : http://www.militarytimes.com/story/military/2016/05/17/isis-loses-45-percent-territory-iraq-20-percent-syria/84512408).

- CENTCOM Embroiled in Climate of Fear (URL : http://www.thedailybeast.com/articles/2016/03/14/centcom-embroiled-in-climate-of-fear.html).

- House passes policy bill for intelligence agencies (URL: http://thehill.com/blogs/floor-action/house/281085-house-passes-policy-bill-for-intelligence-agencies).

- Experts fear US abandoning Syrian rebels (URL : http://thehill.com/policy/defense/270101-experts-fear-us-abandoning-syrian-rebels).

3. ISIS fight: a fresh reboot to the US's economic Supremacy

- McCain: ISIS fight becoming another Vietnam (URL : http://www.militarytimes.com/story/military/2016/04/05/mccain-isis-vietnam-grinding-fight/82663834).

- Weak U.S. strategy is making ISIS stronger, congressman says (URL : http://www.militarytimes.com/story/military/2016/05 /19/weak-us-strategy-making-isis-stronger-congressman-says/84620774).

- House votes to label ISIS attacks as genocide (URL : http://thehill.com/blogs/floor-action/house/272976-house-votes-to-label-isis-attacks-as-genocide).

- To what degree is the the "Defense" industry driving foreign policy? And why Obama is the military contractor's best friend (URL: http://www.againstcronycapitalism.org/2015/05/to-what-degree-is-the-the-defense-industry-driving-foreign-policy-and-why-obama-is-the-military-contractors-best-friend/).

- US lobby backed by arms industry could influence foreign policy (URL: http://www.middleeasteye.net/news/ us-lobby-backed-arms-industry-could-play-significant-role-shaping-foreign-policy-607512040).

- Latest US arms sales to Saudi Arabia raise eyebrows about Islamic State war (URL: http://www.middleeasteye.net/news /saudi-arabia-1295679323

-GOP senator: Apple is 'company of choice for terrorists' (URL: http://thehill.com/policy/cybersecurity/269858-gop-senator-apple-is-company-of-choice-for-terrorists).

- Apple defends China moves amid FBI spat (URL: http://thehill.com/ policy/cybersecurity/273629-apple-defends-china-moves-amid-fbi-spat).

- Military hits snag in Silicon Valley recruitment (URL: http:// thehill.com/policy/cybersecurity/271895-military-hits-snag-in-silicon-valley-recruitment).

- NSA head: Encryption helped Paris attackers hide plans (URL: http:/thehill.com/policy/cybersecurity/269880-nsa-head encryption-helped-paris-attackers-hide-plans).

- What's Behind the Battle Between FBI and Apple (URL: http://dailysignal.com/2016/02/24/whats-behind-the-battle-between-fbi-and-apple/).

4. ISIS presence: a 'tour de force' in geo-economic

- Why China supports Assad : Asian Jihad hits Syria (URL: http://www.transatlanticacademy.org/node/611).

- Does China truly support Bashar al-Assad? (URL: http:/ /english.alarabiya.net/views/2012/02/16/194981.html).

- Why China is reluctant to join the fight against ISIS (URL: http://www.ejinsight.com/20160617-why-china-is-reluctant-to-join-the-fight-against-isis).

- Pentagon Stunned As Thousands Of Chinese Troops Enter ISIS War (URL: http://dailyoccupation.com/2016 /10/07/pentagon-stunned -thousands-chinese-troops-enter-isis-war/).

- Revealed: China's Blueprint for Building Middle East Relations (URL:http://thediplomat.com/2016/01/revealed-chinas-blueprint-for-building-middle-east-relations).

- China's New Era of Diplomacy: Engaging in Syria (URL: http://thediplomat.com/2016/01/chinas-new-era-of-diplomacy-engaging-in-syria/).

- Maybe Putin's Telling the Truth About Winning Syria (URL : http://www.thedailybeast.com/articles/2016/03/15/maybe-putin-s-telling-the-truth-about-winning-syria.html).

- How ISIS Takes Revenge on Russia (URL : http://www.thedailybeast.com/articles/2016/02/19/how-isis-takes-revenge-on-russia.html).

- 'Terminator down': Russian losses in Syria's quagmire mount (URL : https://www.alaraby.co.uk/english/indepth/2016/8/2/terminator-down-russian-losses-in-syrias-quagmire-mount?utm_campaign= magnet&utm_source=article_page&utm_medium=related_articles).

- How will the war in Syria affect the Russian economy? (URL : http://rbth.com/opinion/2015/10/14/how_will_the_war_in_syria_affect_the_russian_economy_50071.html).

- U.S. and Russia Agree on Steps to Combat ISIS in Syria (URL : http://www.nytimes.com/2016/07/16/world/middleeast/us-and-russia-agree-on-steps-to-combat-isis-in-syria.html?_r=0).

- Russia and US 'planning military coordination against Isis in Syria' (URL : https://www.theguardian.com/world/2016/mar_/30/russia-and-us-planning-military-coordination-against-isis-in-syria).

- Kerry Demands Russian Cooperation in War against ISIS (URL : http://en.alalam.ir/news/1838318).

- US to Russia: Syria military cooperation not guaranteed (URL : http://www.foxnews.com/us/2016/09/16/us-to-russia-syria-military-cooperation-not-guaranteed.html).

- John Kerry's latest plan for closer US-Russian cooperation in Syria is getting ripped apart (URL : http://uk.businessinsider.com/john-kerry-us-russia-syria-cooperation-plan-questioned-2016-7?r=US&IR=T).

- Top U.S. commander skeptical of military cooperation with Russia in Syria (URL : http://www.cbsnews.com/news/top-us-commander-skeptical-of-military-cooperation-with-russia-in-syria/).

- U.S. believes Russia purposefully bombed secret U.S. base in Syria to force Washington's hand (URL : http://www.washingtontimes.com/ news/2016/jul/23/us-believes-russia-purposefully-bombed-secret-us-b/).

5. US: the best safeguard of freedom of expression

- Should the United States Ban the Islamic State From Facebook? (URL: http://foreignpolicy.com/2016/01/05/should-the-united-states-ban-the-islamic-state-from-facebook/).

- DoD launches aggressive cyberwar against ISIS (URL : http://www.militarytimes.com/story/military/tech/2016/02/26/dod-launches-aggressive-cyberwar-against-isis/80973470/).

- ISIS supporters threaten Facebook, Twitter (URL : http://thehill.com/blogs/blog-briefing-room/news/270692-isis-supporters-target-facebook-twitter).

- Why Facebook and Twitter Can't Just Wipe Out ISIS Online (URL : https://www.wired.com/2015/11/facebook-and-twitter-face-tough-choices-as-isis-exploits-social-media/).

- White House Forms "Dream Team" To Combat ISIS On Social Media (URL : https://www.fastcompany.com/3057165/white-house-assembling-tech-dream-team-to-combat-isis-on-social-media?utm_content=buffereae93&utm_medium=social&utm_source=twitter.com&utm_campaign=buffer).

- Panel casts doubt on U.S. propaganda efforts against ISIS (URL: https://www.washingtonpost.com/world/national-security/panel-casts-doubt-on-us-propaganda-efforts-against-isis/2015/12/02).

- Anonymous accuses Silicon Valley firm of helping ISIS by protecting their websites from cyberattacks (URL : http://www.dailymail.co.uk/ news/article3338580/Anonymous-accuses-Silicon-Valley-firm-helping-ISIS-protecting-websites-cyber-attacks.html).

- A Wave of the Watch List, and Speech Disappears (URL : http://www.nytimes.com/2008/03/04/us/04bar.html?_r=3&scp=1&sq=liptak&st=nyt&oref=slogin&oref=slogin).

- WikiLeaks website pulled by Amazon after US political pressure (URL : https://www.theguardian.com/media/2010/dec/01/wikileaks-website-cables-servers-amazon).

- Lawless, tyrannical FCC refuses to appear before Congress; "We make up our own laws!" (URL : http://www.naturalnews.com/

048778_Net_Neutrality_Federal_Communications_Commission_government_bureau cracy.html).

- U.S. Center to Battle Islamic State Online Coming to Malaysia (URL : https://www.bloomberg.com/news/articles/2016-07-13/u-s-center-to-battle-islamic-state-online-coming-to-malaysia).

- Online censorship in the states (URL : https://www.aclu.org/other/ online-censorship-states).

6. Well instrumented, ISIS fight is a differentiation element

- Congress' failure to vote on new AUMF against Islamic State would be the real blank check (URL : http://thehill.com/blogs/congress-blog/homeland-security/237095-congress-failure-to-vote-on-new-aumf-against-islamic).

- Give President Obama What He Needs (URL: http://www. redstate.com/erick/2015/02/17/give-president-obama-what-he-needs/).

- Congress Rejected the AUMF Against ISIS Because it Didn't Want a Third Obama Term (URL: http://www.nationalreview.com/ corner/428532/congress-rejected-aumf-against-isis-because-it-didnt-want-third-obama-term).

- Calls Grow to Reject AUMF That Permits 'Waging War All Over World' (URL: http://www.commondreams.org/news/2015/ 02/13/calls-grow-reject-aumf-permits-waging-war-all-over-world).

- Orlando massacre inflames Trump-Clinton presidential race (URL:http://thehill.com/homenews/campaign/283219-orlan do-massacre-inflames-trump-clinton-presidential-race).

- 49 killed in shooting at Florida nightclub in possible act of Islamic terror (URL: http://www.foxnews.com/us/2016/06/12/ florida-authorities-say-multiple-people-have-been-shot-at-orlando-nightclub.html).

- Durbin calls for Congress to pass gun control laws (URL: http://thehill.com/blogs/blog-briefing-room/news/283215-durbin-calls-for-congress-to-pass-gun-control-laws).

- Obama decries Orlando shooting as an 'act of terror' (URL: http://www.militarytimes.com/story/military/capitol-hill/2016 /06/12/obama-decries-orlando-shooting-act-terror/85794630).

- Orlando shooting follows ISIS call for U.S. Ramadan attacks (URL:http://edition.cnn.com/2016/06/13/us/orlando-shooting-isis-ramadan-attacks/).

- Seymour M. Hersh on US intelligence sharing in the Syrian war (URL : http://www.lrb.co.uk/v38/n01/seymour-m-hersh/military-to-military).

- Why former Pentagon chief Chuck Hagel's coming out against the White House matters (URL : https://www.washingtonpost.com/news/checkpoint/wp/2015/12/19/why-former-pentagon-chief-chuck-hagels-coming-out-against-the-white-house-matters/).

- No Republican wants to admit it, but their ISIS strategies are largely the same as Obama's (URL: http://www.vox.com /2015/12/16/10296842/republican-debate-isis).

- Trump Moves from Isolationist to Interventionist (URL : http://www.huffingtonpost.com/entry/trump-moves-from-isolationist-to-interventionist_us_58c7ad6fe4b0d06aa6580477)

- ISIS War Generals to Congress: We Need the State Department (URL : http://www.defenseone.com/politics/2017/03/isis-war-generals-congress-we-need-state-department/136051)

- America's Foreign-Policy Voice Is Fracturing. Trump's Cuts Would Make Things Worse (URL : http://www.defenseone.com/ideas/2017/04/americas-foreign-policy-voice-fracturing-trumps-cuts-will-make-things-worse/136644/?oref=d-mostread)

7. ISIS: A crisis which will last.

- Clapper doubts Mosul can be retaken from ISIS this year (URL: http://thehill.com/policy/defense/279524-dni-doubts-mosul-can-be-retaken-from-isis-this-year).

- ISIS Is Losing Ground, but Not the War (URL : http://www.thedailybeast.com/articles/2016/04/05/isis-is-losing-ground-but-not-the-war.html).

- The Empty Threat of 'Boots on the Ground' (URL : http://www.nytimes.com/2016/01/10/magazine/the-empty-threat-of-boots-on-the-ground.html?_r=1).